A SOLDIER'S BEST FRIEND

Acknowledgements

Amid Javelin missiles, Stealth helicopters and all of the ultra-modern paraphernalia of contemporary war, the anti-modernity of a lone soldier and her dog facing life and death on the battlefield was a timeless story which had to be told.

It is no exaggeration to say this truly has been a labour of love. I was mesmerised by the stories of these dog teams. I only hope I have done them justice.

This book would not have been possible without Lynda's help. She provided a sympathetic ear as well as first class copyediting skills. Her patience and indulgence of my irritating foibles is also much appreciated.

I cannot thank Lesley Martin enough. She is a great photographer and a true friend. It was a delight to work with her in Afghanistan where I got the idea for this book.

Thanks to the Rowe family who opened their home and their hearts to me. I am forever in their debt for all their time and support. I am also grateful to all the handlers, past and present, who were so enthusiastic about this project. Their commitment and enthusiasm kept me going.

Thanks also to Mick McConnell whose courage and determination are an example to us all.

I am indebted to the Daily Record newspaper and the Army press office for allowing me to see Afghanistan first hand.

They gave me the opportunity to go to Kandahar to see the Afghan campaign on the ground. The troops of 3 SCOTS, Third Battalion, Royal Regiment of Scotland, known to history as The Black Watch, are phenomenal soldiers but also proved to be incredibly helpful and kind individuals. Thanks to 7 SCOTS also for their patience.

Many thanks to snappers Phil Dye and Gillian Shaw for their support. Captain Harry Hood was a first class guide through the vagaries of Camp Roberts at Kandahar Air Field and made us feel completely at home. Captain Paul Dargavel also went out of his way to help Lesley and me during our embed.

Media staff and MoD police officers at Faslane were wonderful to work with. As always, they were professional, dedicated and more than willing to help at all times.

A great deal of credit is also due to Dave Harding, John Tucker and the veterans of the Army Dog Unit Northern Ireland. They were not only a great source of information and support but a real inspiration. Author Maria Goodavage is a wonderful journalist who is very generous with her time, a boon to budding writers. Soldier Kevin Hanrahan deserves thanks not only for his exemplary military service in Afghanistan but for his willingness to help get the story of hero dog teams to a wider audience.

Lisa Rogak's work in America is wonderful testimony to the courage, love and loyalty of that nation's military working dogs.

Writer and military expert Niall Edworthy was a great help to me, always on hand with tips and advice. Thanks again are due to Robert Davidson and everyone at Sandstone Press for their professionalism, dedication and support. Last but not least by a long shot, thanks also to Robert and Gerard for their banter, support and most importantly, their questionable curry expertise.

Preface: My confession

'The contrast between the natural beauty and the danger ingrains itself so deep inside you that the feeling doesn't ever leave you.'
Red Army soldier Private Ruslan Yurievich Bezborodov on Afghanistan.

A Black Watch soldier, squat like a rugby player with a stubbly scalp and forearms bigger than my thighs, guides me through the khaki hubbub of Kandahar Air Field. I am blissfully unaware that I am now on a journey which will change my life. I never suspect as I wade through the fine, dusty sand that I will soon meet a young handler and his dog and that they will trigger this book. My eyes will be opened and I will see, first hand, how the war in Afghanistan is the story of my generation, a conflict that has changed the people who fight there and their families at home beyond recognition.

Afghanistan has been the scene of our toughest fighting since World War Two. As I write, more than 400 British soldiers have been killed and I have come to see that military working dogs and their soldier handlers are the spearhead of a massive military effort to minimise casualties and that, without them, the toll would be much higher.

My trip to this beautiful yet terrifying country was a true epiphany, and I feel privileged to have watched our soldiers doing what they are so highly trained to do, namely wage a campaign against some of the fiercest insurgents the world has ever seen. It should never be forgotten that the Taliban and their cohorts accomplished a feat that Hitler and his Panzers could not: vanquishing the might of the Soviet Union's Red Army.

Before going any further, I have a confession to make. I am not a dog owner. I have not yet experienced the joy of gnawed shoes and steaming 'presents' left all over the carpet. I like dogs and would love to have one someday but current work commitments mean I can't at the present time. Critics may say this disqualifies me from writing a book like this about military working dogs and the soldiers who work with them. Of course, I would disagree. Who better to give a fair, impartial assessment of their input to the war in Afghanistan than someone who has never experienced the joys of a pooper scooper or had an expensive leather couch chewed to bits by a rampaging puppy?

Our dog teams are at the forefront of Britain's military efforts in Afghanistan simply because they have to be. The nature of their job means they go out ahead of the troops, sniffing for any dangers that may await, buried in the ground. Estimates vary but some experts believe each dog saves the lives of between 150 and 1800 soldiers in the course of its working life. It is amazing to think that the attention seeking Lab, that slobbers all over you before flopping in front of the fire, is a potential hero capable of saving more troops than many Victoria Cross winners.

These dogs are well equipped for their job. I asked the Ministry of Defence for the kit list that dogs and their handlers use when deployed. A few weeks later, I was emailed sheet after sheet of equipment lists, from obvious items such as harnesses and leashes, to the more bizarre such as doggles and bootees.

The dogs even have their own 'cool coats' which are soaked in water to keep them comfortable while on operations in hot climates, and are issued with 'mutt muffs', specially designed ear defenders to prevent hearing damage.

As I write these words, defence chiefs have just confirmed that it is 'first in, last out' for our military dog teams in Afghanistan. Lieutenant Colonel Mike Purnell is head of the procurement team that selects dogs for the frontline. Dogs, for him, are 'a key lifesaving capability and a key part of force protection for a patrol. Troop numbers will be withdrawn from Afghanistan in the next two years quicker than dog numbers. The dog will have a role in Afghanistan right to the end.'

A number of additional dog teams have already been sent to Afghanistan, deemed as 'Urgent Operational Requirements'. He added: 'It's an emotive subject too. You would not normally describe a dog as equipment and people get very upset when you describe them as such. The dog is an animal and it has equipment around it to support it. They don't live with their handlers; they are not pets, they are working dogs. We have invested in the best first aid and make it available at forward locations. Full vet support is available at Camp Bastion and the dogs go through the same evacuation chain as the soldiers. We don't take shortcuts on animal welfare. We think they are great dogs and it is marvellous to watch them doing their work.'

My own experience confirms that dogs are a top priority in the armed forces. No expense is spared to ensure that they are at the top of their game and I was hugely impressed by the care lavished on our hero dogs both at home and in Afghanistan. The Army maintains the highest standards in veterinary care for both humane and utilitarian reasons, to ensure that dogs are fighting fit. A surge in demand in the last few years has led to even higher standards of veterinary care.

All dogs entering military service undergo a veterinary

examination, not only to ensure that they are fit to deploy on operations but also to provide statistical data which will support future 'health improvement and procurement strategies'.

Veterinary examinations have three phases: gait evaluation, full clinical examination including analysis of limbs and spine and a radiographic examination of hips and elbow joints. Army chiefs can reject a dog at any stage for a number of reasons including cardiac murmurs, glaucoma, pannus, cataracts, and arthritis. Hip dysplasia is the most common reason for dogs being rejected from initial training.

Army medics are highly trained, skilled soldiers able to save the lives of fellow troops in the most traumatic conditions imaginable. Nowadays they are also dual trained, able to treat four legged soldiers on the battlefield. Army vet Captain Tom Roffe-Silvester looks after scores of dogs at his clinic at Camp Bastion, Afghanistan. He told me: 'Obviously, in an emergency, humans are always given priority but, in Afghanistan, military working dogs are given treatment that is just as good. They are trained to an extremely high standard. When the dog finds weapons, drugs or an improvised explosive device, it gives an indication to its handler by sitting or standing up. There are hundreds of dogs in the Army and their service is essential. To ensure they are acclimatised to the heat they get two weeks to get used to the temperatures. We also take care of their paws as the terrain is much harsher there than in the United Kingdom or Germany. We even have specially made boots for them to deal with the terrain.'

He said handlers were also trained in first aid and can deal with heat illnesses, allergies, burns, poisonings and fractures. He added: 'Our vet clinic at Camp Bastion is staffed by a nurse and a veterinary technician at all times. When the handler is given a period of rest and recuperation, the dog is given a health assessment and rest. In Afghanistan, dogs save dozens of lives every day of the week. As well as sniffing out bombs and weapons, they can be trained to find drugs – the main source of cash for the Taliban.'

These wonderful animals also provide a morale boost, winning a place in the hearts of soldiers and civilians alike. During the writing of this book, I was touched to receive many supportive letters and emails from serving and retired handlers as well as animal loving members of the public. Julie Taylor-Radcliffe sent me an email that gave me a major boost as I set about the daunting task of writing.

Julie and her dog Echo were friends of a remarkable lady called Margaret Barker who campaigned from childhood into her eighties for a tribute to animals who fought alongside humans. Julie wrote: 'I just had to get in touch with you. Thank goodness somebody in this country is going to write about military working dogs. I have been campaigning for four years on behalf of the late Margaret Barker to get these wonderful animals the recognition they deserve at Remembrance Day. It was whilst researching the subject I came to realise just how many animals of all kinds went to war, what a benefit they were to morale and how much the dogs are doing today.'

Margaret attended the opening of a memorial to service animals in Dartmouth Park, near Leeds, in April 2011, having fought for this touching tribute since her youth. Just a week later, she passed away peacefully in her sleep. Julie said: 'With Margaret's passing, I am very much a lone voice in this so I get rather excited when I come across somebody like you.'

She sent me pictures of the sculpture which features images of dogs, cats, birds and horses.

A stone sits in front of the memorial with a poem written by Julie. It reads: 'To love unconditionally, to serve unquestion-ably, to trust beyond endurance. Bearing no malice, loyal and protective. They work, play, live, share, enrich, fight and die for us and with us, asking little in return. They are the animals. Oh that man could live by this creed also.'

A line underneath her poem quotes from Vietnam veteran and US scout dog handler John Burnam. It reads: 'I have often thought that worse than dying in a war, is to be forgotten.' I hope this book, *A Soldier's Best Friend*, ensures our dog handlers and their four legged heroes are never forgotten.

A SOLDIER'S BEST FRIEND

The canine heroes of Afghanistan

Stephen Paul Stewart

SANDSTONEPRESS
HIGHLAND | SCOTLAND

First published in Great Britain
and the United States of America by
Sandstone Press Ltd
PO Box 5725
One High Street
Dingwall
Ross-shire
IV15 9WJ
Scotland.

www.sandstonepress.com

Editor: Robert Davidson
Copy Editor: Jane Angus
Indexer: Jane Angus

The publisher acknowledges support from
Creative Scotland towards publication of this volume.

ISBN: 978-1-910124-12-3
ISBNe: 978-1-910124-13-0

Jacket design by Gravemaker + Scott, Amsterdam
Typeset by Iolaire Typesetting, Newtonmore.
Printed and bound by Martin's the Printers, Berwick upon Tweed

For Mum, Dad, Gran and Alex.

This book is dedicated to all serving and former dog handlers in British and coalition forces who have been killed or wounded in action or training.

God and the soldier all men adore
In time of trouble and no more
For when war is over and all things righted
God is neglected and the old soldiers slighted
To absent friends . . .

Contents

List of Illustrations

1. Mick McConnell and Memphis get ready for another day on the frontline in Afghanistan. *Pic: Mick McConnell.*

2. Gearing up: Soldiers, fully laden with ammo and kit, troop on to a Chinook helicopter, known as the workhorse of Afghanistan. *Pic: Lesley Martin.*

3. Benji, an ace arms and explosives search dog, enjoys a break from his daily routine. He wears a sweat rag soaked in water around his neck to help cool him down. *Pic: Lesley Martin.*

4. American and British troops settle in for a long ride home on a Chinook after an operation into the Afghan 'Heart of Darkness'. *Pic: Lesley Martin.*

5. Taste of home: Benji and the soldiers of 3 SCOTS, The Black Watch, enjoy some parcels, packed with goodies, sent from wellwishers in the UK. *Pic: Lesley Martin.*

6. Doggy treats: Benji and his handler Pte Buckland enjoy a treat from one of the many welfare parcels sent to troops on the frontline. *Pic: Lesley Martin.*

7. Defensive positions: Black Watch troops spread out to await their ride back to Kandahar Air Field. *Pic: Lesley Martin.*

8. Dawn departure: A pair of Chinook choppers swoop in low to pick up soldiers after another successful surgical strike on the Taliban. *Pic: Lesley Martin.*

9. Skills and drills: Soldiers practice their clearance drills on an empty compound in Kandahar. *Pic: Lesley Martin.*

10. Calm before the storm: The author and photographer Lesley Martin pictured at the rear of the Chinook which will take them into the Sangin Valley during Operation Tyruna. *Pic: Author's own*

11. Soldiers 'take a knee', crouching down to keep a low profile as they patrol the badlands of Afghanistan. *Pic: Lesley Martin.*

12. Brown out!: A chopper creates a massive sandstorm as it swoops down into the desert to pick up weary troops. *Pic: Lesley Martin*

13. Dogs are traditionally seen as 'unclean' animals by some people in Afghanistan. Sadly, they are often used in organised dog fights. *Pic: Daily Record.*

14. A soldier uses his Vallon metal detector to search for possible roadside bombs also known as improvised explosive devices (IEDs). *Pic: Lesley Martin.*

15. A sad eyed search dog peers into the camera as his handler 'daddy' enjoys some well deserved down time. *Pic: Gillian Shaw.*

16. Canines - such as this search dog - use panting to keep cool especially in the extreme Afghan heat. Note the long lead to give the dog room to manoeuvre. *Pic: Daily Record/ Trinity Mirror*

17. A soldier carries his four legged buddy in the desert heat. Soldiers sometimes have to carry their dogs over walls, fences and other obstacles to help them get access to compounds. *Pic: US Army, courtesy of Kevin Hanrahan.*

28. A Black Watch soldier trudges through an eye catching field of poppies. Opium from the poppies is used to fund the Taliban. *Pic: Gillian Shaw.*

29. Working dog Ryky - who serves with the US Army's 1st Cavalry Division - has a rest at the end of another gruelling patrol. *Pic: US Army, Sgt Mary Phillips.*

30. Military dog Major Butch ends her tour of duty at Bagram Airfield, Parwan province, Afghanistan in 2013. *Pic: US Army, Maj Charles Patterson.*

31. Military working dog Luca goes for a ride during a training exercise at Forward Operating Base Spin Boldak, Kandahar province. *Pic: US Army, Sgt Michael Needham.*

32. Ken Rowe and his beloved Sasha among the sand dunes of Afghanistan. *Pic: The Rowe family.*

33. Ken and Sasha are among the fallen heroes commemorated at the Jigsaw memorial, near his family home outside Newcastle. *Pic: Author's own.*

34. A plaque at the Jigsaw memorial outlines the monument's meaning. It was erected in September 2000 by Sappers from the Royal Engineers. *Pic: Author's own.*

35. A close up of the People's Dispensary for Sick Animal (PDSA) Dickin Medal. It is the highest award an animal can receive for gallantry while serving in a conflict. *Pic: Sgt Adrian Harlen. MOD/Crown Copyright 2014.*

36. US Army 1st Sgt Chris Lalonde, center, holds his military working dog Sgt Maj Fosco, while jumpmaster Kirby Rodriguez, behind them, deploys his parachute during the military's first tandem airborne jump from an altitude of twelve thousand five hundred feet. *Pic: US Army, Sgt Vince Vander Maarel.*

37. Retired bomb busting dog Harry still holds his dignified military bearing after his years in the Army. After his

exemplary service, he was adopted by his hero handler Luke Pryce. *Pic: Author's own.*

47. Soldiers scramble out of a Mastiff armoured vehicle in Kandahar, Afghanistan as they prepare for another mission into the badlands. *Pic: Lesley Martin.*

48. Female medics served with The Black Watch as they battled the Taliban. One female medic gave the author a crash course in emergency treatment before he embarked on Op Tyruna. *Pic: Lesley Martin.*

49. A row of patches on the coat of Katya, 52nd Security Forces Squadron military working dog, during a K-9 unit demonstration. Katya has been with her handler Staff Sgt Shannon Hennessy for two years. *Pic: US Air Force. Airman 1st Class Gustavo Castillo.*

50. A female soldier sports the famous red hackle of 3 SCOTS, The Black Watch at Camp Roberts, Kandahar Air Field, Afghanistan. *Pic: Lesley Martin.*

51. Dogs have a number of roles in the Army. Conmeal, a two-year-old Irish Wolfhound is the regimental mascot of 1st Battalion Irish Guards. *Pic: Sgt Ian Houlding RLC. MOD/Crown Copyright 2014.*

52. Mick McConnell, his partner Lorna and Memphis are enjoying a new life together after their horrific experiences on the frontline in Afghanistan. *Pic: courtesy of Mick McConnell.*

Cover images:

Front: Sgt Rupert Frere RLC. *MOD Crown Copyright 2014*

Back cover photograph *Pic: courtesy of Gillian Shaw*

ONE

Memphis chases the dragon

Memphis strains on the leash ahead of his daddy, Mick McConnell. The inseparable pair are on another frontline mission in Afghanistan, boldly stepping into the Taliban's backyard. Springer Spaniel Memphis and his handler are like a parent and child. Memphis is the inquisitive, energetic kid and Mick the older, wiser, father figure ready to scold him, if necessary, for trying to pinch a morsel from another soldier's rations.

When Mick gets Memphis into his harness though, he knows it's time to work. Before each patrol, Mick must keep him calm and focussed since his performance means the difference between life and death for dozens of people. Like thousands of other dogs, Memphis has been given a vital role by the Army, locating IEDs (Improvised Explosive Devices).

Now, trudging slowly and methodically through an area dubbed 'the most dangerous square mile in the world', every step is checked and cautiously taken knowing it could be their last. This is Nad-e-Ali, the centre of Taliban territory, dubbed the Heart of Darkness. As inhospitable as it is, insurgents will fight to the death to keep their stranglehold on this stretch of desolation in a corner of Helmand. In 2012 alone, seven coalition soldiers were killed and 25 gravely injured defending this spot, Checkpoint Toki.

Mick and Memphis are the 'tip of the spear', out in front, on point, clearing the way and making sure that the terrain is safe, or made safe. Memphis's nose twitches as he glances at Mick, sniffing the desert breeze that blows across the dry riverbed in front of them. The pitted moonscape around them is burnt solid by thousands of years of searing sunshine. In parts, the ground is hard as glass. Elsewhere the fine sand resembles ochre talcum powder.

Mick takes off his helmet to mop his forehead. Tall, willowy running to thin, with a sensible, well-tended haircut, he looks more like a bank manager or an accountant than the stereotypical image of a soldier as brawny, close cropped tough guy. The pair work with the elite Royal Marine commandos, a crack fighting unit that prides itself on outstanding fitness, discipline and always taking the fight to the enemy.

During basic training, Mick learned that Memphis and other working dogs enjoy a far superior range of senses to humans. Canine combatants have a powerful armoury at their disposal, such as a moist nose that helps dissolve scent molecules giving dogs a rich, multi-layered awareness of their environment. He also learned that dogs have two billion olfactory receptors in their nose compared to just forty million in humans. One dog handler summed it up this way: 'There are certain things, like the dogs' sense of smell, their sight, and their hearing, that is way more in tune. You might be out on a patrol, and to you it looks like a normal road; and then your dog, it lets you know that: hey, there is something not right here! Their sense of smell is so good. For instance, a cheeseburger. We might only smell the cheese or the burger, but they smell the cheese, the pickle, the tomato and the lettuce. It's almost as if they get it in 3-D.'

Memphis and his four legged comrades also enjoy wider peripheral and clearer night vision. They sense movement better than humans, and their hearing is vastly superior, allowing them to hear sounds their two legged pals can't even make out. These are the reasons Mick trusted Memphis so implicitly.

As the sun blazes down, Mick splashes water on the dog's coat to provide at least some respite from the unrelenting heat. The drops from his black plastic water bottle wet Memphis's dappled coat, leaving it darker as the fluid evaporates. Meanwhile, his canine pal's senses buzz with the whiff of unwashed human bodies, the faint industrial odour of oiled rifles, the rank smell of raw sewage and the sharp, piercing brightness of ground which is scorched almost white in places. Such a sensory assault could overwhelm a less experienced dog.

They tread carefully. The next step could be their last as every inch of the ground is potentially seeded with IEDs. Memphis's training means he knows when he is inching nearer to his target and, by extension his favourite ball, his reward for a job well done.

Suddenly he catches an unfamiliar smell, human, but not the sweaty body of a tired squaddie. There is no cloying smell of deodorant or acrid stench of tobacco. This one is strangely different from the normal battery of odours he scents from British soldiers every day in Helmand. It is also very close, perhaps just thirty metres away.

Memphis builds what experts call a 'scent picture' of his environment. The multi-layered aromas that his nose picks up are beyond the reach of any human, the residual signature smell of a Taliban bomb maker. A heady human cocktail of stale sweat, dead skin cells and bodily oils lingers on roadside bombs even if they have been buried in the ground days before. A red flag is raised in his brain – something is not right. He must warn his daddy and get his reward. With his head flicking from left to right, he puts his muzzle to the ground to find the exact source.

3

Without warning, a massive elemental force, like a hurricane, hurls the dog across the ground like a rag doll, whimpering as a wave of stones, grit and sand is thrown into his eyes and muzzle. Scrabbling to his feet, Memphis scampers around in circles trying to see and smell his daddy, Mick. After the initial shock-wave, as the cloud of dust and sand begins to settle, he is wide-eyed, scouring the field where Mick last was.

Among the gusts of white smoke, he sees a pile of rags and his nose is assaulted by a cloying metallic smell. He runs back and forwards, terrified and unsure what to do. Where is daddy? What is happening? If he could speak, he would be screaming at the top of his lungs. He hears other men shouting and runs to them, sees the shape of a man who looks like his daddy lying prostrate, staring unblinking into the sky. The man thrashes his arms, moans something that Memphis can't make out. Through the legs of the other soldiers he watches them unwrap lengths of material that he has never seen before, placing them on the man's leg.

This can't be his daddy. He smells the same, and looks similar, but Memphis has never seen him behave in such a strange way. The man is trying to prop himself up on his elbow, looking at the bottom of his leg which has been transformed into a red, ragged looking piece of meat. Marines pull him onto a stretcher, preparing him for the helicopter and emergency medical treatment.

Through the searing pain and shock, Mick regains his senses enough to see his beloved Memphis. A marine is holding him by his harness. As he is carried away, he reaches to give his canine partner a scratch behind the ear, to calm him, but Memphis – a look of wide eyed horror in his eyes – wriggles free and bolts, looking for somewhere, anywhere, to hide.

TWO

MWDs unleashed

Crouching on wiry legs, huddled together as dusk falls, these men have slung the tools of their trade, battered AK47 assault rifles, effortlessly over their shoulders on frayed slings. They wear black turbans with loose ends tied around their faces. As their debate becomes more heated their voices rise and fall until the sun disappears behind their ramshackle compound. They have the furrowed faces of world weary elders but are probably only in their thirties and forties. Old age is relative in a country as harsh as Afghanistan.

These fighters defeated the Red Army, a feat that Hitler and his Panzer Divisions could not manage, but they meet today in this desolate corner of Helmand Province to face a new problem which threatens to derail their campaign of killing and maiming British and American soldiers. These Taliban fighters have one thing on their minds: dogs. More specifically, military working dogs.

These so-called 'Soldiers of God' have a terrifyingly effective weapon in their arsenal, the roadside bomb or IED. The Taliban, the name derives from the Pashto for students, are some of the most effective insurgents in the world. Canny enough to understand they have little chance when taking on well-armed, specially equipped regular troops in a stand up fight, they rely on the homemade bomb.

The British Army responds with its own secret weapon. Remarkably, it is a weapon that has been under our noses for years, the tousled, unkempt, four legged pet that is such a commonplace member of our families, the dog. Across Afghanistan, the Taliban hold crisis summits to combat the remarkable dogs that have uncovered so many of their IEDs, hunted so many of their fighters, and smashed their supply lines by discovering tonnes of weapons and ammunition; and the drugs that provide vital funding for their war effort.

In another part of Afghanistan, I met Kevin, the Army's newest poster boy, who tilted his head for the camera, to display teeth that glisten in the sun like chunks of white marble. After years of the best military training in the world, his every move is disciplined and each step shows off his taut muscular frame. His deep brown eyes sparkle and he is clean and well groomed, testament to the finest food and care that money can buy.

Much to the embarrassment of the Army's top brass, Kevin has some character flaws, such as slobbering, and an unfortunate tendency to sniff his private parts at inopportune moments. He has his own minder, a blog read by thousands of people, and is at the spearhead of one of the British Army's newest and busiest regiments. He is also a Belgian Shepherd. Like Memphis, he is a military working dog, and a fellow graduate of the world's leading military dog school, the Defence Animal Centre in the Midlands of England, a high-assurance search dog who can sniff out roadside bombs and weapons caches. Three quarters of all NATO casualties in Afghanistan have been caused by IEDs.

War tests soldiers, mentally and physically, beyond breaking point. The sights, sounds and visceral, stomach churning experience of modern combat are unlike anything in other walks of life, but for dogs like Kevin and Memphis it is just a big game. When a working dog searches out a stash of drugs, a bomb or a human, he knows that he will get his reward, a tasty treat, a rubber chew toy, or even a rolled up pair of socks to play with.

When I first started to research this book, I was struck by how these dogs are a breed apart. Some may well have the playful good looks and wagging tail of a family pet, but they are highly trained, disciplined, working animals with thousands of people relying on their every move. I was to discover that stricken British dogs on the front line are given the same medical priority as a wounded soldier.

Training and equipping a working dog from whimpering puppy to deployable four legged soldier costs up to £30,000, but dogs are one of the few military assets that increase in value as they age. The Pentagon is the world's biggest spender on military working dogs, having shelled out nearly $19 billion on space age bomb detector technology in 2010 only to find that dogs remain their most effective defence against roadside bombs. Cutting edge equipment such as drones only have a detection rate of 50 percent while dogs are effective more than 80 percent of the time.

It has taken decades for the military establishment to recognise how important they are, but times are indeed changing, and now the British Army has created a special military working dog regiment.

It's not hard to see why these dogs are so effective: loyal and intelligent, speedy, these qualities are in addition to their sensory superiority. NATO and the British military today use them in a variety of roles including protection, vehicle search, arms and explosives search, drug detection and infantry patrol.

In the Vietnam War, dogs were used only as four-legged weapons to guard bases, patrol sites and hunt the enemy, but the British Army in particular has learned from past experience and uses all of the main classifications of dogs on operations in Afghanistan. Deployed breeds include German Shepherds, Border Collies, Labradors and Springer Spaniels. Like the

Americans and Australians, the British often deploy Belgian Malinois.

Some are employed in protection and patrol, reducing the need for soldiers to be taken from the battlefield and used as security personnel. Trained to be aggressive, these dogs chase and stop intruders in their tracks and, in military parlance, are classed as 'force multipliers'.

Arms and explosive search dogs are trained to indicate the presence of arms, explosives and other weapons in all types of buildings. They can also search vehicles, cars, lorries, trains, ships, containers and aircraft for weapons and explosives.

Vehicle search dogs are used at checkpoints and in facilities which handle high numbers of vehicles. According to Army documents, these dogs are 'generally deployed on permanent or snap vehicle check points, at camp entrances, border crossing points and sea borne operations.'

Tracker dogs are used after an incident where suspects may have fled on foot. They are useful because intelligence can be gained about the direction of flight, which in turn can point to forensic evidence, such as footprints or tyre marks.

Protection dogs, also known as guard dogs, are another useful canine weapon, on patrol as well as in guarding bases, but only certain types make the grade and are considered suitable for the rigours of a protection dog's job. Herding breeds such as German Shepherds and Belgian Malinois tend to be the dog of choice for this kind of work. Rottweilers were deployed in the past but gained a reputation for being lazy, with a weaker bite than other breeds.

Today's military working dog programme effectively employs expertly trained and motivated handlers coupled with highly intelligent breeds of dogs. These teams are continuously rotating between their assigned duties and worldwide deployments to perform joint operations, multi-echelon tasks and inter-agency missions.

For decades, it was the sniper that every infantryman feared and loathed. The soldier's most feared enemy was seen as sneaky, cold blooded and undiscriminating, but IEDs are the bogeyman for ground troops in Afghanistan. Hidden in roads, dry riverbeds and even built into walls, any piece of roadside rubbish might be attached to a hundred-pound bomb. They are the troops' worst nightmare. A routine patrol in what was thought to be a safe area can be transformed in a millisecond into a glimpse of hell. One step in the wrong direction can mean instant death, and failing to do something as simple as following in another person's footsteps can lead to disaster.

The IED threat in Afghanistan cannot be underestimated. Taliban booby traps, Soviet era mines and the detritus of decades of war litter the countryside, making Afghanistan the most dangerous place on earth. The Army has developed many counter tactics, from Vallon metal detectors to ultra-secret electronic devices designed to prevent detonation, but Kevin and his four legged comrades remain its best resource in finding and eliminating these terror weapons. A soldier who is lucky enough to survive an IED strike has just four and a half minutes before bleeding to death.

Former Parachute Regiment officer Sean Rayment told me that the image of a fanatical lone bomber methodically producing IEDs is out of date. He said: 'IEDs are now being manufactured on an industrial scale. It is no longer a cottage industry. Bomb factories in some parts of Helmand can produce one every fifteen minutes. Made from pieces of wood, old batteries and home-made explosives, they are basic and deadly. The Taliban have already produced IEDs with low metal or no metal content which are difficult to detect, so, as well as using equipment to detect bombs, troops also need to rely on what they call the 'Mark One' eyeball, hoping to spot ground signs.'

Between September 2009 and April 2010, there were almost

2000 IED incidents. Between 2001 and the time of writing, there were 3395 coalition deaths in Afghanistan. More than 2100 Americans have died in the war while 445 British and 40 Australian soldiers have been killed in action.

More than 5200 soldiers have been admitted to British field hospitals for serious combat injuries including traumatic amputations. All other participating NATO countries, such as the US, Australia, Estonia and Germany, have suffered similar numbers of casualties. In an average week in February 2010, 200 IEDs were detonated or discovered by dog teams and bomb disposal experts. That is 10,400 IEDs a year, more than one for each British soldier in Afghanistan.

The climate is another problem for soldiers and their dogs. Before any thought can be given to training or combat, both have to be acclimatised. Kevin and his kennel mates go on exercise in warm countries, such as Kenya and Jordan, to prepare them for the rigours of Helmand's unrelenting heat, where fifty-degree temperatures bake the province's featureless landscape.

Handler Lance Corporal Kelly Wolstencroft joined Kevin months before they set off for Afghanistan in 2011, and writes a blog about him and his new role on Operation Herrick, the military name for operations in Afghanistan.

Her first tour of duty in 2008 saw her working as a vehicle search dog handler. She was then deployed in 2011 as a high assurance search dog handler. Despite the stress of her job, Kevin always raises her spirits. She says: 'If Kevin isn't breaking into my locker and ripping up every t-shirt I brought with me, you'll be sure to find him dragging one of the counter IED searchers across a checkpoint by the goggles.'

Like all handlers, Kelly always puts Kevin first, attending to his needs before she even thinks about eating or grabbing a five minute rest. Kevin has a burgeoning online following thanks to his blog but his story is not unique, and I was to hear countless stories of dogs like Memphis and Kevin leading the charge on the frontline.

Molly is one such, a quiet hero that most people have never heard about. With the long, floppy ears and brown, mournful eyes that are the trademark of English Springer Spaniels, Molly is one of the toughest military operators in the Army and thinks nothing of working ten hours, straight, on the frontline.

With 45 kilogrammes of body armour, webbing and supplies strapped across her body, Molly's handler looks like any other squaddie, but she is a highly trained veterinary assistant who manages a captivating smile despite the excruciating heat. Private Charlotte Cook is 21-years-old and a long way from home in Borehamwood, Hertfordshire. Cookie, as she is known by pals, says, 'Before this I was very much a Labrador person but now I am very definitely for the Spaniels. They are so resilient.'

Molly almost leapt into Cookie's arms when she first walked into her kennel. Sometimes, a handler and a dog can take a while before they hit it off but these two were a great match from the start, and it took only two search operations before they were working in perfect harmony. It is very unusual for any dog to do five tours of duty but she has proved to be a wonder dog in the face of the enemy.

Together they have made scores of finds: including sniffing out a suspected booby trap, quantities of ammunition and a huge cache of fertiliser, one of the main ingredients in Taliban bombs, the same kind that was used by Provisional IRA bombers in the 1970s and 80s. She adds: 'The dogs are always tremendous morale lifters for the soldiers. They looked after me well, the soldiers, pulling me out of ditches. I am only five foot three and the Afghans found me pretty weird at first. They just stared, but then couldn't stop talking to me. I couldn't understand, but the little girls would come and hug me, and loved playing with my plait. They are mostly good people, but the bad people hate and fear the dogs.'

Cookie has had a number of close shaves. While she was waiting outside a compound in the countryside, the Taliban lobbed four grenades over the wall. She suffered shrapnel wounds across her arms but fearless Molly never once left her side.

Like all dog handlers, Cookie has to carry Molly's kit as well as her own. On an average patrol, she takes a spare lead, harness, about fifteen litres of water, tennis balls for Molly to play with, bowls, food for them both, and a washbag, as well as a weapon and ammunition.

I was in the newsroom when the phone rang with news of one of Molly's final missions in Afghanistan. The distortion and time delay on the line told me immediately that the call was coming direct from the Army's media operations Head Quarters in Lashkar Gah, meaning it had to be a big story. Molly had again come up trumps, spearheading a five-day blitz by Scottish soldiers on the Taliban's tribal heartland.

She and Cookie had led a strike by troops of 4 SCOTS, The Highlanders, into one of the deadliest parts of Helmand province. Molly was drafted to sniff out booby trap bombs ahead of the soldiers as they moved into the infamous Loy Check region, a lawless area that had become a byword for heroin production and Taliban activity.

Soldiers had set off from their base before dawn carrying a back breaking fifty kilos of kit. The troops, normally based in Fallingbostel, Germany, were welcomed by locals as they plodded through villages. One local father told soldiers that his four-year-old son had been shot in the face by insurgents.

Cookie says: 'The only problem with Molly on operations like this is she's a bit of water baby and loves to have a swim but, when she's cooled off, she's ready to get on with the job. Everyone who gets to know Molly trusts her instincts. She's a great dog.'

Molly and her kennel mates have even attracted celebrity followers. Popstar Cheryl Cole is one of many stars to travel to Afghanistan, where she was hugely impressed by the dog soldiers. She arrived in Helmand Province in 2011 to mark ten years of British operations in the country, having boarded a troop carrier aircraft at RAF Brize Norton in Oxfordshire for a twelve-hour flight, and having previously undergone hostile environment training to prepare her for the trip.

Cheryl was treated to several military working dog displays during her high profile stay at Camp Bastion. She said: 'Afghanistan was an unbelievable experience. The whole trip was incredible. The men and women I met out there were inspirational, and so amazingly brave and dedicated.'

In September 2011, Molly, one of Britain's longest serving four legged soldiers, went on a well-deserved spot of leave, having just completed her fifth tour in Helmand.

Memphis, Kevin and Molly are just some of the extraordinary animals that make the transition from rescue dog to army recruit every year, often plucked from a life of neglect and misery to be given a new start with a rewarding career.

Dogs are sometimes given to the armed forces because they are just too much for their owners to handle. One such is Treo, a cheeky, energetic Labrador, who proved too boisterous and temperamental for his civilian owners. Despite his youthful exuberance, he forged a phenomenal army career, winning the animal version of the Victoria Cross.

Treo's handler, Dave Heyhoe, developed a deep bond with the black Lab from the first moment they worked together. After forming a huge respect for working dogs in tours of Bosnia and Northern Ireland he heard tales of a gifted Labrador who was destined for great things. There was a snag though, Treo had a fearsome temper and a bark to match.

After years of being a tough infanteer Dave knew a challenge when he saw one. He approached the kennel with caution but was determined to show Treo who was boss. He should not have worried. From the first day, the dog was like putty in his hands. Dave quickly matched his over-exuberance with lots of exercise and, soon, Treo's possessiveness about his food faded. This was the start of a fruitful nine year career together. Being presented to the Army by his original owners, the Abbot family from Bristol, gave Treo just the lease of life he needed, an outlet for his boundless energy and boisterous nature.

In September 2007 the two, who are so tightly bonded that 'it's difficult to see where the dog ends and the man begins', got word that they were to be posted to Afghanistan. Treo, like all his four legged comrades, already recognised the scent of ammunition and explosives but the all-pervading dust would present a new challenge.

Army chiefs use quarries to test the dogs, a scent object hidden and the dogs deployed to detect it among the sand and dust. Treo excelled, and showed no signs of concern when he left the depths of an English winter for the scorching cauldron of Sangin valley, where waves of Taliban fighters routinely attacked British positions in the small towns of Musa Qala, Sangin and Now Zad. Taliban leaders were determined to hold the area with a constant barrage of AK47 machine guns, rocket propelled grenades (RPGs), and hidden IEDs.

Dave used spent RPGs and old pieces of weapons to train Treo before they went out on a mission, and Treo's trusty tennis ball was never far away, his reward. They did not have to wait too long for their first taste of battle.

Two days after arrival, Treo was on patrol with a crack unit of Royal Marines. After a day of searching, compound after compound, the heat and tension started to take their toll in weariness and patience. Then the stillness of the afternoon was torn apart by automatic arms. Dave tied Treo to a post and returned fire until the gun battle subsided when Apache attack helicopters arrived. Through it all, Treo acquitted himself well, staying calm, almost looking as if he could fall asleep while gunfire raged around him.

Working on the end of a long leash, known as a pilot line, Treo would search for and find buried rocket propelled grenades and roadside bombs, signalling their presence by sitting down or wagging his tail. In August 2008, he hit the jackpot, a chilling new type of booby trap bomb which the metal detectors and fancy electronic gear had missed. It was a daisy chain IED, a device linked to several others to cause maximum loss of life. It had even been fitted with an anti-tamper device designed to blow up anyone who tried to defuse it. Treo saved many soldiers' lives in that one mission. In September 2008, he again located an IED, saving scores more from death or severe injury.

A United State Marine Corps officer who witnessed Treo's work was so impressed that he felt moved to write an official commendation. Master Sergeant Tanos Chaves, of the Explosive Ordnance Disposal team, who worked closely with British military dogs, wrote: 'The skill of Treo is unsurpassed by any military working dog I have ever had the pleasure of working with. I believe that Treo saved lives by locating IEDs.'

Pentagon chiefs say dogs are vital weapons against roadside bombs in Afghanistan. A dizzying range of technology from unmanned aerial vehicles, ground-penetrating radar for low-metallic explosive devices, robots and roller systems have been used to combat the deadly IED, but the team of soldier and bomb-sniffing dog is still the best. The US military elite have even admitted the folly of their previous use of military working dogs. In their newest field manual, Pentagon chiefs reveal: '. . . military working dog teams are employed in dynamic ways never before imagined. Today's military working dog team is a highly deployable capability that commanders have used around the world from Afghanistan to Africa and the Balkans to Iraq. These specialised teams aid commanders in stability and support operations as well as in war fighting.'

Taliban fighters loathe working dogs, especially highly

successful ones such as Treo. As his tour went on, and he proved himself time and again, we learned that he was a so-called 'high value target' for the Insurgency. Intelligence sources revealed that he was attracting attention that could endanger his life. Insurgents had started broadcasting the warning: 'The black dog is out. Beware. The black dog is out.'

Treo made it home safely from the war and in August 2009 retired from the army to become Dave's pet. The following year, Dave received the overwhelming news that Treo had won the People's Dispensary for Sick Animals (PDSA) Dickin medal, the animals' Victoria Cross. His original owners, the Abbott family, were at the ceremony in the Imperial War Museum in London to cheer him on.

During their six months in Helmand Province, Treo had been faultless. He was, in Dave's words, 'a true soldier friend.' Treo has now settled to the life of a pampered pooch and lives with Dave in comfortable retirement in Lincolnshire, but the work of serving military dogs Memphis, Kevin and Molly continues.

The forerunners of these dogs cut their teeth in the forbidding streets and fields of Northern Ireland during the Troubles. Thanks to decades of experience dealing with the IRA's hardened bombers, the British Army's experience of combating IEDs is second to none.

In military speak, the war in Afghanistan, as in Northern Ireland, is a counter-insurgency campaign, a mission to win the hearts and minds of locals while cutting off support and supplies from the rebel fighters. Military dogs are the perfect counter IED weapon for this type of campaign. They are efficient, cheap and do not cause collateral damage to civilians.

Experience gained at a heavy price on the tough streets of Derry and Belfast has given Kevin, Treo, Molly and the other graduates of the Royal Army Veterinary Corp's handling courses an unprecedented level of expertise in bomb detection. This superior training led to one difficult Belgian Shepherd called Chocolat going from being unable to sit on command to cracking a bomb-making production line in the space of only a few months.

In 2010 Chocolat uncovered a stash of homemade explosives, old claymore mines and enough equipment to make ten IEDs during Operation Moshtarak, a major offensive against the Taliban, sniffing the haul inside an open shop front during the search of a bazaar in the Nad-e-Ali. His handler, Private Steve Purdy, said: 'Chocolat totally right-angled, went in, and wouldn't come back. Normally he would never go out of my sight. It was enough for me to pull him back and report with confidence that there was something there. That's how sure I was.'

The search team inched through the claustrophobic compounds of the bazaar with weapons ready to take out any Taliban fighters preparing to make a last stand. Another large explosive was found but a bomb disposal expert called a halt as he felt the 'atmospherics' were not quite right. In civilian terms, he sensed a trap. After Chocolat cleared a route at the back of the buildings the team blew a hole through a compacted mud wall and discovered that an area at the front had been set up to kill troops with hidden IEDs.

Private Purdy said: 'Chocolat's success at finding IEDs in the initial few weeks of Operation Moshtarak was impressive. The troops really value him and his search capability. He is really helping to save the lives of some key players in the dangerous world of counter IED.'

Troops know that the finely tuned nose of a bomb-sniffing black Labrador can mean the difference between life and death in Afghanistan. According to US Marine Corps handler Corporal Andrew Guzman, the dogs are more reliable than

17

any machine. 'They are 98 percent accurate. We trust these dogs more than we do metal detectors and mine sweepers.'

Across the Nato coalition, a number of dogs have found fame for their outstanding service. Brooks, a three year-old Labrador with tan fur, deployed three times in Iraq and Afghanistan with US forces, helped recover at least fourteen bombs. Another dog, Ringo, gained a legendary reputation for having found as many as thirty daisy-chain landmines in Iraq.

The need for these dogs was made clear, had it not been before, when the number of roadside-bomb incidents in Afghanistan soared from 2,677 in 2007 to 8,994 in 2009 and 10,500 in 2010.

A skilled soldier and dog are game changers, and billions have been invested in training since the Afghan conflict began. The British Army recognised their importance in a landmark move in March 2010. For the first time in military history, the brave dogs and their equally heroic handlers were formed into their own regiment when Army chiefs created the 1st Military Working Dog Regiment. Crowds flocked to see the inaugural parade and skill demonstrations at the unit's main base in Sennelager, Germany.

Over the years, the soaring demand for military working dogs led to the creation of five independent units which saw action in Bosnia, Kosovo, Northern Ireland, Iraq and Afghanistan. The hero dogs of 101, 102, 103, 104 and 105 Military Working Dog Support Units were amalgamated to form the new regiment which comprises 284 soldiers and officers and about 200 dogs. This was a historic move – dog teams are now recognised as a major military asset in their own right rather than an auxiliary rear echelon unit.

Headquarters are at Chiron Barracks but units are spread across the UK and Germany. Its primary role is to provide specialist military working dogs and veterinary support to troops out on the ground.

These dogs will continue to be at the cutting edge of Britain's wars for a long time to come, searching out and helping to clear routes, buildings and vehicles. In addition to their search role our four legged friends will help guard and patrol key installations, enhance base security and 'provide a range of other capabilities wherever they are needed in the rest of the world'.

Wherever they go the dogs give a sense of assurance, a tremendous morale boost, and a remembrance of home to young soldiers. In Afghanistan, officers are proud that the dogs and their human colleagues are saving lives every day in the toughest conditions in the world.

Colonel Jonathan Welch, who commands 29 Explosive Ordnance Disposal and Search Group, explained the significance of this regiment: 'It demonstrates the vital contribution that all the military working dog sub-units are making to the campaign in Afghanistan. The provision of detection and protection capabilities combined with wider veterinary support is adding real value to current operations, especially in combating IEDs.'

In Afghanistan the role of military dogs is dynamic and constantly evolving. Just as insurgent tactics develop over time, they and their handlers are constantly being used in new, challenging ways. There is a striking irony at work here. Hardline Islamists such as the Taliban consider dogs to be dirty and 'un-Islamic', fit only to be used as fighting dogs or ill-treated sentries. Yet, it is these same dogs that have proven to be their most effective foe.

Back in a barren, rural corner of Helmand, crouching, deep in conversation, the assembled Taliban chieftains now puff on cigarettes. Mingled with the cheap, illicit tobacco, they can almost taste the bitter fear of failure in the back of their throats. Their secret summit has drawn a blank. Yet again they have failed to find a way to outwit their biggest bane, the military working dog.

Our four legged soldiers are the best in the world. In time, my life would depend on them.

THREE

My gamble

'Nothing is so exhilarating in life as to be shot at without result.'

Winston Churchill.

KANDAHAR, AFGHANISTAN: August 2009.

Dying is easy. Surviving after being blinded and horrifically maimed is the tougher option. I am weighing up what could happen to me. Coming here is the biggest gamble of my life.

My mind races as our flight descends towards its final destination. Adding to my growing unease, the lights flicker and go out, plunging us into total darkness. This is the signal to put on our helmets. The aging RAF Tristar starts to dip and weave and I am not sure if this is turbulence or the pilot's tactic to dodge incoming missiles.

My stomach groans with a combination of grinding nervousness and the lurching of the aircraft, and I look around at the silhouettes of helmeted soldiers sitting in row after row. The silence is striking, no-one speaks, coughs or even moves, there is no banter, no gallows humour. This is it: welcome to Afghanistan.

My trip would become an epiphany: a nerve shredding glimpse of life on the frontline and an insight into the importance of military working dogs. The brooding silence on the plane, however, was oppressive, only adding to my justifiable anxiety. We had been flying for hours and were on the final run in to Kandahar Air Field, Afghanistan, or KAF as the troops know it.

The flight was far from comfortable. I am not a great flyer at the best of times and soon spotted that this plane was well past its prime. My photographer, Lesley Martin and I, boarded at RAF Brize Norton in Oxfordshire after a sleepless night in a local hotel, on our way to Afghanistan to be embedded with British troops, and the last few days had been spent checking and re-checking our kit: laptops, cameras, satellite phones. The MoD has booked us on a flight but we could be shunted off at any time due to the changing military situation in 'Afghan', as the troops refer to the country which now dominates the headlines.

Having boarded after an interminable wait with hundreds of squaddies either returning from R and R (Rest and Recuperation) or going out to start their tours of duty, we settled in for the long flight. I was shocked by the state of the plane's interior: plastic panelling that was cracked and hanging off, seats battered and deflated. The fleet of prehistoric Tristars was originally owned by British Airways and Pan Am and picked up by the RAF in the early 1980s. They remain largely unchanged from their airline days, carrying up to 266 passengers.

We sip fruit squash served by RAF personnel in dashing pink jumpsuits.

Conditions in the plane provide a welcome distraction from thinking too long about where we are going. Lesley and I will be embedded with a famous unit, namely 3 SCOTS, The Black Watch, an infantry battalion of the Royal Regiment of Scotland, for a few weeks. Our stay will be nothing compared to the six month tours that the troops have to endure. The strain on the military of fighting such a vicious campaign in Afghanistan means that many soldiers are doing one tour of duty every 18 months or so.

Our approach into Kandahar is made at night, another tactic designed to frustrate any Taliban gunman determined to bring down the plane. Thankfully, our landing is uneventful but, when the cabin doors open, the heat strikes us like a sledgehammer. It feels like standing inside a blast furnace. Family holidays to the Costa Brava and the Algarve never had heat like this. We are shepherded on to local buses, each decorated with bells, trinkets and baubles on the front grill, indicating the idiosyncratic panache of the driver.

I am already becoming familiar with the infamous Afghan sand. We are in the country only minutes yet we are already covered in a fine, dusty layer with the consistency of talcum powder. It penetrates our clothes, shoes, even our nostrils and I develop a hacking, spluttering cough for the duration of my stay.

As the buses wheeze into life, we gaze onto the landing strip to watch lines of troops file patiently onto hulking Chinook helicopters, soldiers about to take off on another mission. Each group is headed by a working dog and its handler. The animals seems perfectly in tune with their humans; their every move appears to be in perfect harmony. The dogs are content, obedient with no words spoken. It seems that, almost instinctively, they know what is expected of them.

In soldiers' parlance, their 'skills and drills' are first rate. I had visions of military dogs straining at the leash, growling, barking and yelping at everything that moved, but there is nothing like that here. The dogs exude calmness and control despite the roar of Army vehicles, helicopters, jets and the incessant to-ing and fro-ing of every bit of military hardware known to mankind.

Their handlers look equally relaxed and at ease despite the

fact that they must lead the way on each mission. By the very nature of their job, arms and explosive search dogs and their handlers have to be at the forefront of the unit, keeping an eye open, and a well-honed, damp nose stretched out for any IED that can cause carnage in a millisecond.

As our buses roar off into the deepening night, heading for the Central Arrivals Point, I understand that image of the dogs and their handlers, patiently waiting to go into the badlands, to risk their lives, will live within me for a long time.

Next day, our first stop is Camp Roberts, home of 3 SCOTS, also known as 3rd Battalion of the Royal Regiment of Scotland, or the famous Black Watch. Effectively this is an army base within a base. The large lion rampant next to the front gate signifies that we are in the right place to meet the men and women of the legendary British infantry unit. The Black Watch remains one of the best known units of the British Army, having won battle honours around the world from Waterloo to the Somme to Monte Cassino. These soldiers have a big reputation to live up to.

As always in this country, decimated by decades of war, the name of the camp carries great significance. Camp Roberts is named after Major Alexis Roberts who was killed in October 2007. The 32-year-old father of two is famed for his role as Prince William's platoon commander at Sandhurst military academy, and is yet another victim of the ubiquitous IEDs. His vehicle triggered a roadside device on the way back to Kandahar Airfield after a successful operation. At the time, he was the most senior British Army officer to die in Afghanistan.

We are given a larger than life escort in the form Captain Harry Hood who leads us around the camp. He is a 6ft 4in career soldier who made his way through the ranks and commands the respect of everyone we met. His pallid Scottish complexion, burnished by the scorching sun, adds to his fierce look. He is a barrel chested, imposing officer who knows the job of soldiering intimately.

I originally fear that his occasional quiet spells mean the lifelong Dunfermline Athletic fan, with his thick Fife brogue, isn't too keen on journalists sticking their noses into Army business. However, after a few days he will become more of a friend than a military guide. As he tours around the camp, we notice the flags are at half-mast and we are told in hushed tones that 'Op Minimise' is in effect. When a soldier is killed in action all communication between troops and the outside world is shut down for 24 hours. The purpose is clear, to stop information about the fatality leaking out before next of kin can be informed and supported.

We would hear the crackling monotone of 'Op Minimise, Op Minimise' coming over the camp's tannoy system more times than I care to remember over the next few weeks. Staying at Kandahar Airfield is an almost surreal experience, especially for the soldiers. One minute you can be munching on a sandwich in a Subway fast food store, or having an ice cream while shopping for locally made carpets and trinkets. An hour or so later you might be deep in what the troops call the 'Heart of Darkness', in the most dangerous places on the planet with hordes of highly trained, well equipped Taliban fighters doing their best to end your life.

The clash between the comforts of western civilisation and the realities of modern warfare is very stark. The wooden boardwalk area with its alcohol free cafes, shops and Pizza Hut is located in the middle of the base and attracts soldiers at all times of the day and night. Most of the British soldiers I speak to prefer to be based at KAF before flying out on airborne assault missions and being whisked back again by Chinook helicopters, usually at dawn. Here, they are guaranteed running water, proper toilets and other mod cons rather than having to stay in a rudimentary Forward Operating Base, or FOB as they are known. FOBs can be very basic with latrines which have to be emptied each day. The human waste is then drenched in fuel and burned, a malodorous task which soldiers hope to avoid during their tour.

Despite the colossal size of the base, which is home to some 30,000 military and civilian staff, and the huge security operation around its perimeter, it is far from completely safe. One soldier wag told us that KAF is an impenetrable superbase like 'Heathrow in the desert with guns', but the place is still very much prone to rocket attack, as we would learn only too well.

One night, as we filed our story and pictures for the next day's paper, we heard the sirens dotted around the base start to wail and loudspeakers calmly announcing, 'rocket attack, rocket attack!' Photographer Lesley and I stood dumbfounded in the media operations room in the centre of the base even though we had been instructed several times on what we should do in such a terrifying situation.

Our British Army minders took control of the situation and got us moving as we struggled to put on our cumbersome body armour and helmets. We moved quickly away from the windows and lay on the floor. After what seemed like an eternity, but must have been just minutes, the all clear siren sounded and it was back to business as usual. As soldiers returned to their duties, I felt rather punch drunk, taking about 15 minutes to eventually regain a semblance of composure and get my wobbly legs functioning properly.

A US Army officer told me these attacks used to occur only once every few weeks, but were now happening several times a night or at least every few nights. He said: 'They fire them from the mountains to the northwest and sometimes they hit pretty close. After the siren sounds you only have a few seconds before the rocket arrives and they rarely fire multiples. At night the aim for the lights, and most of the lights are here near the boardwalk. They mean to hit the runway or the flight line, but they usually way over or undershoot. They are certainly trying their luck more often.'

A few nights later, we were back at the boardwalk for a concert for troops of the multi-national International Security Assistance Force (ISAF) which includes Britain and the US. In so doing, we were about to see for ourselves the depth of the challenge facing NATO in Afghanistan. The concert was shrouded in secrecy with details of where and when it would be held only released at the last minute. Despite the security measures, the ochre, sun blasted social centre yet again came under attack. Within minutes of the concert starting, the siren roared and thousands of soldiers flung themselves into the dirt. After the all clear, everyone dusted themselves off and carried on as normal but, a few minutes later, we came under attack again. Every inch of the wooden boardwalk's floor became very familiar to me as I wallowed in the dust, hugging the ground for dear life.

Many of the soldiers looked insouciant on all-clear, swarming back to the concert or making their way into the carpet stores, coffee shops and huge tax-free PX stores that sell everything from laptop computers to cigarettes, sweets, DVDs, magazines and clothing. I couldn't help thinking: was this a fluke? It seems odd that the Taliban managed to guess the time and place of the concert. Or was someone, a local worker perhaps, feeding them information. It was a sobering thought as we headed for our portakabin-style accommodation and a troubled night's sleep.

After a day or two getting our bearings and sunning ourselves among the throngs of troops and contractors at the boardwalk, we are back at Camp Roberts to meet one of the battalion's key players.

Benji, an adolescent black Labrador, is fearless. Unlike

27

Kevin and Private Kelly Wollstonecraft he doesn't have his own blog, followed by thousands of readers online, but his precious nose has helped to snare dozens of Taliban fighters and taken tonnes of IEDs from the streets and alleyways of Helmand Province.

His unstinting devotion and selfless heroism is at the heart of the war on terror but he is also pivotal in the other forgotten conflict in Afghanistan, the war against drugs. Using his years of training, he has helped clear the way for soldiers to net mountains of opium and heroin which had been destined for the West. Benji is just one of hundreds of dogs on the frontline, facing the same trials and tribulations as British soldiers and their international allies in Afghanistan. Their contribution to this counter-insurgency campaign is colossal and, as I learn to my horror, largely overlooked.

Pte Buckland's fair hair is bleached to the colour of straw by the unrelenting sun that pounds down from around 4.00 am. Benji, meanwhile, looks sleek, fit and eager, although the oppressive heat makes him so tired he relaxes in the shade whenever he gets any down time. Like the soldiers, Benji has lost weight due to the desert conditions and the constant high tempo of his work on operations. His ribs are visible through his dewy, ebony coat which is beaded with perspiration and the water that Pte Buckland douses him with to keep him cool. Benji and his fellow military working dogs in Afghanistan eat very well but their furious work rate means they burn a prodigious amount of calories. Their human comrades also get noticeably thinner thanks to patrols where they carry weapons, body armour and eighty-pound packs crammed with water, food and ammunition.

We go to a central area within Camp Roberts, an open space of parched dusty land that has been turned into a training area and a car park for dozens of Mastiff, Jackals and other armoured vehicles. The old cliche is true: you can literally fry an egg on the armour of a Mastiff armoured vehicles, and a few of the troops we meet have done just that in the middle of the dasht, or desert.

As we crouch in the only available shade, behind a wall of Hesco Bastion, the ubiquitous fortifications that line every part of the landscape, we watch as Benji is put through his paces. With his tail wagging, he criss-crosses the berms of the training area in search of his quarry, a small sample of explosives. Within minutes, he is on the scent, winning the prize of his favourite rubber ball after he passively indicates the correct site of the potential IED.

With his English accent and RAVC background, handler Pte Buckland stands out from most of the other Black Watch soldiers, who tend to come from Fife or Dundee, although he and Benji have seamlessly become part of the team. After Benji trots off for a well-earned drink and a rest underneath a parked Mastiff vehicle, we meet the battalion's padre, David Anderson.

The padre is a young looking forty something, eager to give me a guided tour of the camp. He tells me that dogs, such as Benji, have an invaluable practical role as well as a tremendous ability to boost morale among soldiers who are far from the comforts and normality of home. He says: 'Benji has been great. He is such a hard worker and we all love to see him around the place. When the guys go out on ops, they see him and know things will be okay. It's great for them, if they are having a hard day they can give Benji a pat and get a bit of warmth and affection back.'

Padre Anderson shows us the hundreds of parcels that are sent to the working dogs from across the UK. Many contain snacks, chews and toys, but they aren't allowed to get their paws on the toys as their training is built entirely around performance and reward. If they get other toys, it may dilute their desire to please their handlers and get to play with their own special toy. Any distractions for Benji will potentially cost lives.

Padre Anderson says: 'Benji is a new addition to us but we have already received welfare parcels for him. Dog lovers in the UK send stuff over like toys, dog treats and sweets. Benji has been spoiled already. It is a challenging environment for him and everyone else here but he just seems to get on with it and do his job. Everybody is just very grateful for all the stuff that gets sent and the fact that we haven't been forgotten about at home.'

It isn't long before we get the chance to see Benji working on the frontline. Just days later, we are invited to sit in on a pre-operation briefing for a mission called Op Tyruna, a surgical strike on a Taliban fortress deep in the much feared Valley of Death, otherwise known as Sangin Valley.

We gather in a tent to listen to senior officers discuss the plan of attack for the following night. As they discuss where the troops will land and their exact movements over the terrain, I have an extreme rush of blood to the head. I find myself sticking my hand up and saying: 'Excuse me, can I go along on this operation?'

An audible gasp goes around the room before the Major in charge of the Black Watch's grenadier company says that he will look into whether I can get the necessary permission. He will get back, he says, still taken aback by my apparent enthusiasm.

In a few hours, I have my answer: 'yes', the top brass have cleared us to go along. I feel elated that I will achieve my goal of getting out from 'behind the wire', but then a surge of doubt kicks in. What am I doing? I must be losing my mind. I now know why there is an adage that you should never volunteer for anything in the Army. I have no idea what makes me go through with it: male pride, reluctance to lose face? Who knows? But I am determined not to pull out now that we have permission. Photographer Lesley confides that she too is nervous, but still wants to go.

After a sleepless night tossing and turning in my Army issue sleeping bag I feel like a condemned man as the clock ticks by and we await our lift to the airstrip. Captain Hood drives us down to the battalion's training areas as his soldiers make their final preparations and we watch as they practise their drills on how to clear compounds, check for IEDs and search for weapon stashes.

Their stamina is admirable as they trot from place to place laden with rifle, bergen rucksack and ammunition. The white heat hammers down on our heads and I feel dizzy just watching them.

At one side of the training area we are given a special crash course in emergency medical procedures in the event of being shot or blown up; shown the different bits of kit, tourniquets, field dressings and an emergency syringe of morphine, that will keep us alive. In a matter of fact way, the 20-year-old female medic from South Africa runs through the drill. She says: 'If your arm or leg is blown off, try to stay calm and attach the tourniquet above the point where it has been severed. Pull it as tight as you can then tighten it with these twists to stop the blood flow.'

As her words sink in, I feel a knot in the pit of my stomach and begin to question my involvement in the whole mission. When she explains how to self-administer morphine with the small syringe, to ease the pain of a traumatic amputation in an IED strike, I feel faint and her lesson on applying field dressings to gaping wounds becomes a queasy, sweaty blur.

Further doubts grow through the day and there is an uneasy tension as we sit in the cookhouse trying to eat. Captain Hood tells me: 'Right, we have a few hours before you need to be down at the airstrip so you should do what the boys are doing, getting their *heids* down ahead of tonight's fun and games.'

We head back to our bunk beds but, needless to say, sleep evades me. Captain Hood helped us pack our daysacks earlier in the day so I sit on my bunk running through everything that should be in there: a bladder and camelbak drinking system with three litres of water, another five litres of bottled water, rations, jelly sweets (good for energy apparently) and a small compact camera.

We have been told this is only going to be a 10 hour op or we would have needed much, much more. I struggle to get the unwieldy pack on my shoulders and marvel about how some of the smaller, lighter soldiers manage with much more gear. We are picked up in a small, white people-carrier and taken closer to the landing strip. It is hard to exaggerate the colossal scale of KAF; the drive takes us ten minutes just to get close to our rendezvous area.

We can hear the roar of the engines as we approach. Dusk hits fast in Afghanistan so, by this time, we are in pitch darkness. We join the soldiers sitting on their bergens, chatting and, in most cases, smoking, and I am reminded of that old, grainy black and white footage of the trenches in World War One with seemingly every soldier smoking cigarettes.

Every man and woman appears to be either smoking a cigarette or, in some officer's cases, a cigar. The odour of tobacco is everywhere and mingles in the night air with the loud conversation of soldiers as each prepares in their own way for the attack. Through the gloom and clouds of smoke, we see young Benji, ears twitching, taking in the noise and the flurry of activity around him but otherwise undisturbed by the aircraft and the mob of humans.

He seems almost preternaturally calm, as if highly attuned to the mood of Pte Buckland who sits with him, quietly looking into the distance. Benji displays his veteran status as the blast from the choppers comes closer and the engine roar grows to a scream, remaining placid but alert. He must have seen this a thousand times: the last minute check of weapons, the scramble to scrutinise ammunition, the lists of names hollered in the darkness.

We get a first look at the chariot that will wing us into the badlands: a US Chinook helicopter. The double rotored choppers are the workhorse of Afghanistan, hauling troops, beans and bullets over massive distances as the roads are so dangerous. They are also one of the Taliban's most prized targets. The insurgents would dearly love to bring one of these aircraft down and one lucky shot could wipe out dozens of troops, destroy a multi-million pound helicopter and signal a colossal propaganda coup for the Taliban.

After an interminable period of waiting, the hour arrives: 22:22 hrs exactly. Time to go.

Benji is alive to the change in tempo. He trots to the rear ramp of the Chinook with Pte Buckland clutching his lead. His eyes dart around but there is no sign of tension as he watches the soldiers tramp on board, placing their weapons downwards so that a stray round is not accidentally fired up into the rotors, potentially bringing down the aircraft. He attracts a few smiles from the troops and the odd ruffle of his fur but seems aloof, aware that this is now work time. He is again at the vanguard of a daring night raid on a Taliban stronghold in the Sangin Valley, 'the most dangerous place in the world for British troops'.

Sangin has long been a focus of coalition efforts given its key role as an economic and transport hub in southern Afghanistan. The Taliban has other plans, and fight tenaciously to maintain its stranglehold over the area. It was the scene of heavy fighting for British forces before being handed over to US troops in September 2010. At one stage of the war, the Sangin valley alone accounted for almost a third of UK deaths.

Benji and Pte Buckland are at the forefront of this airborne surgical strike that intended to hit the Taliban hard, with hundreds of soldiers dropped in during the pitch black Afghan night. On a US helicopter, Lesley and I are surrounded by British and Afghan troops, a testament to the multinational nature of the war. A total of 18 UK, US and Australian helicopters take part. Benji is working with Alpha Company on this huge blitz on the Taliban's narco-terrorism network.

Nine Chinooks, three Black Hawks, two Sea Kings and four Apache attack helicopters tear out of the darkness and sweep across the vast, almost oceanic expanses of open desert. Some 300 SCOTS soldiers, a US Army engineering detachment and scores of crack Afghan troops are taking part. Our target: a heavily guarded Taliban fortress in the small hamlet of Malmand Chinah.

On board, everything is bathed in an eerie, green light. A young US Army gunner looms out of the darkness, skipping over boxes of equipment to take up his post. Complete with a striking, black Darth Vader style dust mask, he rattles off dozens of rounds into the darkness as we prepares to hit the landing zone. Benji barely bats an eyelid but I have to be coaxed down from the ceiling as the bullets roar out into the night just inches from our heads.

Each soldier is impressively tooled up and ready to go. So is Benji in a special harness that is designed to give Pte Buckland full control over his movements while allowing him to wander far and wide in search of weapons and IEDs. The harness is checked to make sure it is secure since a rattle or jangle at a key moment could alert the Taliban.

Everything inside our Chinook workhorse is bizarrely calm as grinning squaddies check their kit again and high-five each other in the occasional bout of bravado. A shaven headed soldier, complete with a tattooed angel glistening through the sweat on his neck, bumps fists with his pal and gives me a broad grin minus two front teeth. As we soar along, I take stock of my surroundings, which seem surreal to a mere civilian like myself.

My gamble

The dull glow inside the chopper illuminates a scene that would make the most bloodthirsty Taliban fanatic weep. I have never seen such an arsenal of modern weaponry crammed into such a tight space. The 'Jocks', as the SCOTS are affectionately known, are armed to the teeth with machine guns, missiles, grenades, sniper rifles, high explosives and good old fashioned bayonets, and it appears that every one of them is looking for a fight. I shudder as I imagine being on the receiving end of this barrage of 21st century muscle power.

I cling to my canvas seat as the lights dim, and eventually fade out completely, and the helicopter lurches in the sky. Once the green night lights are turned off inside the chopper, we are left to brood over what lies ahead. The troops don their night vision goggles.

With stomachs churning, thanks to a combination of nerves and the choppy ride, we are given the nudge and told to prepare to run off as the helicopter touches down at our target. I pull down my ballistic goggles and adjust my helmet, sweating furiously under pounds of body armour. The Chinook blasts down with the rear of the aircraft bucking wildly in the air, flinging the rear gunner to one side and nearly out of the door into the blackness.

It is auditory overload as the rotors whine and splutter. We run off the ramp and onto the parched earth under an 80 mph down blast, to hurl ourselves into a deeply furrowed field. The soldiers sprint to take up defensive positions. It is just another night's work for Benji but I am in danger of hyper-ventilating. With just seconds to catch my breath I take a pull from my water pack before it starts: an Apache helicopter's fearsome chain gun ripping into insurgent positions.

I hear another sound I will never forget, hundreds of crazed dogs barking as the massive column of troops begins to infiltrate the Taliban compounds. A crackle and pop sound, like giant sheets of bubble wrap being twisted and burst, signals incoming small arms fire. The Taliban know we have arrived. On our feet again we make our way through a maze of sun-scorched compounds, all the time making sure we follow directly in the footsteps of the man in front.

My heart seems to leap out of my chest as I round a corner to confront a huge, barking dog as it leaps towards my face. Staggering back, I fall into a clump of needle sharp bushes. The growling terror in front of me has no ears, doubtless hacked off to make him even more fearsome. This is one of the infamous fighting dogs of Afghanistan, brutally maimed and occasionally used as guard dogs. I recoil with my arms flailing as a chain, which I haven't noticed in the pitch darkness, tightens and drags the devilish looking creature back to earth.

We then head to a complex of houses moulded out of the rock hard earth as Benji and the soldiers start their drug and IED searches. Slumped on the ground, we greedily drink water and crunch boiled sweets to maintain our sugar levels as we wait for the houses to be cleared. This is just the start of Benji's shift as he begins to sniff out his quarry.

A white flash followed by a bang shakes me to the core and nearly knocks me over. The Afghan crack units have just made their way into another suspicious building. This time, they decide to go through the wall by blowing a hole in it. Sporadic gunfire breaks out followed by suppressing shots. Tireless Benji goes from house to house sniffing every crevice, eventually striking the jackpot by unearthing a massive haul of weapons and drugs.

His handler, 25-year-old Pte Buckland, would tell me: 'Benji is primarily an arms and explosives dog so he can be used to seek out both. I only picked him up four months ago but he is a great dog. He found a kilo of homemade explosives about a month ago which would be used to make improvised explosive devices. He has found weapons, explosives, you name it. I am not too sure he is that keen on the heat out here. He can really speed things up when we are out on operations and go straight to the drugs or whatever. He is a terrific worker. Finding the explosives for Benji is like a game. When he finds them, he gets his reward, his toy ball. It is work for him but he also enjoys it and has a lot of fun with it too. This is all in a day's work for Benji.'

His training as an arms and explosive search dog is based on modern reward based techniques. The humble tennis ball or simple dog toy is the focus of all the training. Benji is first exposed to the scent of a specific substance that he will track. Each time he finds the targeted scent, he indicates a find by standing still or lying down. The handler then rewards a find by giving the dog its favourite toy. A successful find saves the lives of the soldiers on a patrol but also prevents local men, women and children being killed or injured by these hidden devices.

As dog expert Isabel George says: 'The skill and bravery of these dogs touches hundreds of lives.' On this night, Benji pinpointed a cache of weapons and a massive haul of 250 kilogrammes of wet opium, all of which were destroyed. Smelling his target, Benji tenses up and his whole demeanour changes. He seems purposeful and incredibly alert before lying down in front of his find.

As the night wears on, another massive explosion leaves me reeling, wondering about how we will cope with a rapid two-and-a-half mile march through terrain studded by jagged rocks, deep ravines and, most worryingly, deadly IEDs. After a brief rest, we gather our kit, which includes the remainder of our surprisingly tasty rations, and seven litres of water, and move out in single file to the helicopter landing zone, through a field dotted with booby trap bombs, always fearful that the next step could be our last.

Walking with Benji and Pte Buckland, I am struck by the incongruous beauty of the landscape. It feels like walking on the surface of the moon despite the choppers whooshing over us. Eventually, the moonlight fades and the sun gradually appears from behind the awe inspiring mountains of the Sangin Valley.

Attack helicopters in the air behind us launch a series of chaff and flares, designed to deflect any heat seeking missiles, and as the brightly coloured fireworks die down I realise that we are threading our way past an old cemetery. In Afghanistan, the dead are buried above ground with rocks piled over them to deter scavengers. The rags used as markers above the stone cairns flutter in the wind that sweeps down from the mountains. Normally, this sight would have seemed gruesome but, with dawn drawing closer, it seemed oddly tranquil.

There are no such distractions for Benji, whose job is far from over. As we walk, I spot several small stones stacked into a pyramid, a tell-tale marker used by locals to indicate either IEDs or Soviet era landmines. Benji and his two legged comrades walk in single file in the footsteps of the person in front. We have no time to worry about the possible dangers as we must be at the landing site just after 06.00 hrs for our extraction.

With moments to spare, we arrive at the LZ, or landing zone, kneel down and await the churned up rocks and sand which will herald the Chinooks' arrival. Feeling horrifically exposed we slump on the flat ground at the foot of several mountains. Time seems to telescope and a minute feels like an hour. Benji, of course, maintains his professional composure, sitting tired but relaxed at the feet of Pte Buckland.

After what seems like a lifetime, the roar of a helicopter is heard in the west. Sure enough, our airborne taxis, a fleet of Chinooks, roar in, slamming down a few hundred feet in front of us. Grabbing cameras and rucksacks we run for the rear doors, diving into the chopper, which speeds off in an undulating, defensive manoeuvre to foil any watching Taliban snipers.

It has been a rewarding night's work. Benji and his team located 250 kilogrammes of wet opium, worth more than $1.5m, as well as a cache of deadly weapons that would have been used to target British soldiers, and seven Taliban fighters were killed. One by one, the soldiers on the flight slump on their weapons, drifting into a deep and well deserved sleep.

After the operation, Major Robin Lindsay, who planned the strike, was a happy man. He told me: 'This type of high intensity technique, where we airlift a large number of troops into a small area, effectively storming it, has been shown to work time after time. It proves to the Taliban beyond doubt that they have no safe havens even in the most remote, isolated places. We can hit them at will wherever and whoever they are. The money from the sale of the opium would undoubtedly have funded the insurgents' activities, further strengthening their hold in the area and their ability to launch deadly attacks on coalition forces.'

This strike was eventually immortalised in the battalion's official history. The Black Watch's official account of the 2009 tour called Aviation Assault Battle Group describes the mission thus: 'The battle group successfully disrupted the insurgents in Malmand Chinah through a single wave of aviation assault. Intelligence following the operation suggested that the size and disposition of the ISAF forces and also the continued presence of the Apache helicopters dislocated and disoriented the insurgents and also discouraged insurgents from conducting any form of harassment. Further information derived from local nationals and our intelligence indicated that the bazaar contained a number of IEDs and was a focal point.'

Benji, like his comrades Memphis, Kevin and all the rest, has taken on the Taliban's most fearsome weapon, the IED, and

won. This surgical strike on the Taliban's backyard empha-
sises the importance of our dog teams. I slumped on my Army
bunk bed in the relative safety of KAF feeling like I had won
the lottery. Thanks to Benji, I had made it back to base in one
piece. My gamble had paid off.

FOUR

Fighting back

Mick faces the biggest fight of his life. He is battling to walk again, while fighting the gnawing depression which accompanies his forced separation from Memphis. He was saved by a lucky combination of factors: speedy medical aid, first class body armour and the partial detonation of the device. His ballistic underpants, as the soldiers call them, protect his pelvis and groin area from shrapnel. Mick was on a specially equipped emergency medical helicopter within 14 minutes of the explosion, taken back to Camp Bastion for lifesaving treatment on his lower leg.

He suffered hours of gruelling surgery. At Bastion, doctors operated to reset his dislocated foot before sending him back to Britain to begin his long road to rehabilitation. In the Queen Elizabeth Hospital in Birmingham he is confined to bed for a month, with his foot raised to reduce swelling.

During his spell there, surgeons operate to fix several dislocations and complex fractures to his left foot and ankle. They also remove fragmentation and shrapnel from his right leg and dress the burns caused by the blast. A steady stream of visitors clutching sweets and get well soon cards flock to his bedside and he is bombarded by messages of support from his comrades at home in the UK and on the frontline, but he can't stop thinking about his boy, Memphis. 'Is he ok? Will he come back to me?' Thoughts assail his mind as he lies in his hospital bed, staring out at the hospital's new space age buildings, towering over him in chrome, glass and steel.

Memphis seemed not to recognise Mick at the time of the explosion, so traumatised was he by the blast. The memory of him bolting as Mick was taken away, fills Mick with a sense of utter desolation.

In the immediate aftermath of the bomb blast, the Marines took Memphis under their care. He paces around at night, his food uneaten in his bowl. The shock of the blast combined with the terror of being alone, lost to Mick, leaves him bereft. The marines do their best but have no idea how to make things better. He even turns his nose away from the pieces of ration pack beef jerky they offer.

Mick cannot move from his hospital bed, in this sense his separation from Memphis is truly paralysing. In Afghanistan, they lived, trained and worked together. Now, he isn't even sure where his boy is. He will be well looked after but when, if ever, will he see him again?

Mick has faced adversity before, living in an area of high unemployment and poverty in a deprived area just outside Glasgow, making his way up the ranks, fighting to be deployed on the ground in Afghanistan and then waging war against the Taliban. Now, he knows he must battle to get his boy Memphis back.

1 Mick McConnell and Memphis get ready for another day on the frontline in Afghanistan. Pic: Mick McConnell.

2 Gearing up: Soldiers, fully laden with ammo and kit, troop on to a Chinook helicopter, known as the workhorse of Afghanistan. Pic: Lesley Martin.

3 Benji, an ace arms and explosives search dog, enjoys a break from his daily routine. He wears a sweat rag soaked in water around his neck to help cool him down. Pic: Lesley Martin.

4 American and British troops settle in for a long ride home on a Chinook after an operation into the Afghan 'Heart of Darkness'. Pic: Lesley Martin.

5 Taste of home: Benji and the soldiers of 3 SCOTS, the Black Watch, enjoy some parcels, packed with goodies, sent from wellwishers in the UK. Pic: Lesley Martin.

6 Doggy treats: Benji and his handler Pte Buckland enjoy a treat from one of the many welfare parcels sent to troops on the frontline. Pic: Lesley Martin.

7 Defensive positions: Black Watch troops spread out to await their ride back to Kandahar Air Field. Pic: Lesley Martin.

▲ 9 Skills and drills: Soldiers practice their clearance drills on an empty compound in Kandahar. Pic: Lesley Martin.
◄ 8 Dawn departure: A pair of Chinook choppers swoop in low to pick up soldiers after another successful surgical strike on the Taliban. Pic: Lesley Martin.

10 Calm before the storm: The author and photographer Lesley Martin pictured at the rear of the Chinook which will take them into the Sangin Valley during Operation Tyruna. Pic: author's own.

11 Soldiers 'take a knee', crouching down to keep a low profile as they patrol the badlands of Afghanistan. Pic: Lesley Martin.

12 Brown out!: A chopper creates a massive sandstorm as it swoops down into the desert to pick up weary troops. Pic: Lesley Martin.

13 Dogs are traditionally seen as 'unclean' animals by some people in Afghanistan. Sadly, they are often used in organised dog fights. Pic: Daily Record.

14 A soldier uses his Vallon metal detector to search for possible roadside bombs also known as improvised explosive devices (IEDs). Pic: Lesley Martin.

15 A sad eyed search dog peers into the camera as his handler 'daddy' enjoys some well deserved down time. Pic: Gillian Shaw.

16 Canines – such as this search dog – use panting to keep cool especially
in the extreme Afghan heat. Note the long lead to give the dog room
to manoeuvre. Pic: Daily Record/Trinity Mirror.

17 A soldier carries his four legged buddy in the desert heat. Soldiers sometimes have to carry their dogs over walls, fences and other obstacles to help them get access to compounds. Pic: US Army, courtesy of Kevin Hanrahan.

18 Dogs can get into every nook and cranny to search for bombs and arms caches. This US soldier from the 2nd Infantry Division has let his dog off the lead to check out a crumbling building. Pic: US Army.

19 Pop star Cheryl Cole gives a military working dog a refreshing drink during her visit to Afghanistan in 2011. Pic: Daily Record/Trinity Mirror.

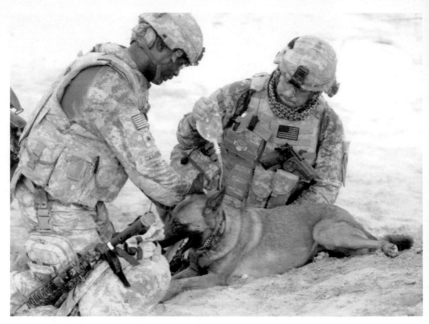

20 Army medic Sgt Laurence Cameron (left) places a lifesaving intravenous drip into a military working dog as Sgt James Harrington helps. Dogs receive the same first class medical care as frontline soldiers. Pic: US Army. Sgt Mary Phillips.

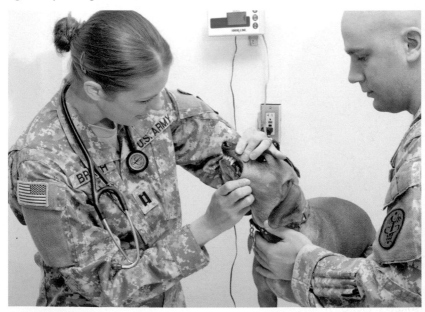

▲ 22 Arms and explosive search dog Bracken was a smash hit at the Defence Animal Centre in Melton Mowbray. Pic author's own.

◀ 21 Military working dogs receive the best veterinary care. Dogs that are wounded in battle receive the same priority casualty treatment as injured soldiers. Pic: US Army.

23 A close up of an MOD search dog, trained in detecting explosives. The Ministry of Defence Police has one of the largest dog sections of all British police forces. Pic Harland Quarrington, MOD, Crown Copyright.

24 Kennel work Alyson Marshall loves her work with the MoD police dogs at Faslane – some of the best trained military police dogs in the UK. Pic: Phil Dye, Daily Record.

25 Handler Pte Buckland tucks into his rations during a patrol in Kandahar as Benji looks on. Pic Gillian Shaw.

26 Author Stephen Stewart during his journalistic embed with 3 SCOTS, The Black Watch in Kandahar. Pic: Lesley Martin.

FIVE

War dogs through history

Memphis and his comrades are now at the vanguard of the fight against the Taliban but their ancestors have been used in warfare for thousands of years. History shows that the bravest soldiers often aren't even human. Man's best friend has served in countless bloody wars, saving lives and boosting morale in equal measure.

Historians and archaeologists have been debating the genesis of domesticated dogs for decades but one thing is beyond any doubt, dogs and their wolf ancestors have been used by humans since prehistoric times and, for as long as dogs have been domesticated, put to use in every conceivable form of warfare.

As author Nigel Allsopp notes, it is unsurprising that two species, human and canine, that are so alike should come to be so closely bonded over the centuries in peace and war. In *Cry Havoc*, he says: 'If I describe an animal that has a shared sense of community, is raised by a mated pair with help from other family members, has a dominant hierarchical society, is organised for a hunt, and territorial . . . I could be talking about man or wolf. No wonder we have shared or competed so much in history. From the beginning, the earliest humans may have selected dogs for their abilities such as guarding and hunting. No animal has served man more nobly than dogs in times of conflict.'

There has been a keen academic debate about exactly when and where dogs were first domesticated by humans. In 2002, scientists from Sweden and China seemed to have solved the problem with pioneering research. Dogs were evolved from wolves in East Asia around 15,000 years ago. Geneticist Peter Savolainen and his team examined the DNA of 654 domestic dogs, representing all major dog populations worldwide, and found patterns indicating that Asia was the cradle of the domestic dog we know and love today. From these obscure origins, domesticated dogs spread around the world to become a vital part of society and an effective weapon of war.

Cave paintings show dogs being used in hunting and warfare well before the development of the written word. Pre-literate societies were quick to see their utility combat. These crude images show dogs as a central part of hunter gatherer societies from Thailand to Africa and Australia. Archaeological excavations also appear to confirm the date of canine domestication at around 15,000 years ago. One of Europe's oldest joint human and dog burials, showing the bond between human and animal some 14,000 years ago, was unearthed at Bonn-Oberkassel in Germany. Meanwhile, the earliest domesticated dog found in China was discovered at the Jiahu burial site in Henan Province which is thought to date from between 7000 to 5800 BC.

Ancient Egyptians revered dogs for their link to the jackal god Anubis. They were even depicted on the reliefs in tombs of Tutankhamun and Rameses the Great. The most famous story of a loyal war dog in the ancient world comes from Homer's epic poem *The Odyssey*, dating from around 800 BC. Odysseus returns home after decades to find his faithful dog Argos on his last legs. Odysseus is in disguise and cannot acknowledge the instant recognition between himself and his four legged warrior.

Book 17 of *The Odyssey* tells us: 'A dog that had been lying asleep raised his head and pricked up his ears. This was Argos, whom Odysseus had bred before setting out for Troy. There was not a wild beast in the forest that could get away from him when he was once on its tracks. But now he has fallen on evil times, for his master is dead and gone, and the women take no care of him. Servants never do their work when their master's hand is no longer over them, for Zeus takes half the goodness out of a man when he makes a slave of him. So saying he entered the well-built mansion, and made straight for the riotous pretenders in the hall. But Argos passed into the darkness of death, now that he had seen his master once more after twenty years.'

Homer also mentions attack dogs, sentries, draught dogs and even messenger dogs equipped with a special collar for carrying dispatches. In other parts of the ancient world, dogs established themselves as a vital part of the warrior's arsenal. In Iraq, Assyrian temple walls show bas reliefs of huge battle dogs wearing spiked iron collars to create fear among their enemies. Roman Legions used large breeds against the barbarian hordes. The Scourge of God himself, none other than Attila the Hun, was also fond of his war dogs. He used packs of large dogs around his encampments to prevent a surprise attack from his many enemies as he drove ever westward into the heart of Europe.

Around the same time, the British used dogs when they attacked the Irish tribes. The Irish used Irish Wolfhounds to attack invading Norman knights on horseback. A single wolfhound was often capable of taking a mounted man in armour off his horse before the dog's lightly armed handler delivered the *coup de grace*.

Pliny the Elder tells us about special units of fighting dogs that fought in the ranks beside the Colophonians of Asia Minor, against their Ionian enemies. After the battle was over, they were harnessed to carts to haul captured treasure back home.

One of the breeds that looms large in the history of war dogs is the Mastiff, an ironic quirk of history given that the British Army has named one of its armoured vehicles in Afghanistan after these pugnacious, four legged warriors.

English Mastiffs were known as 'Pugnaces Britanniae' by the Romans who came to fear their large jaws and bulky build on the battlefield. Opinion is divided on how the Mastiff name came about. Some sources say it came from an Anglo Saxon word 'masty' meaning powerful while others claim it derived from Latin. Either way, the dog was a favourite when it came to violent pastimes. From classical times to the medieval period, they were used in blood sports from bear baiting, bull baiting, to dog fighting and even lion baiting.

Physician John Caius, who later co-founded Gonville and Caius College, Cambridge, gave a detailed description of the dogs and their fierceness in battle in 1570. He points out that the animals feared no-one and 'that no weapons will make him shrink nor abridge his boldness'. His work 'Of Englishe dogges: the diversities, the names, the natures, and the properties' describes the mastiff. The imposing animal was also known as a 'bandogge', a type of guard dog which was bound to its master's house by a sturdy chain.

Caius tell us: 'This kind of dog called a Mastyve or Bandogge is vast, huge, stubborn and eager, of a heavy and burthenous body, and therefore but of little swiftness, terrible, and frightful to behold, and more fierce and fell then any Arcadian curre (notwithstanding they are said to have their generation of the violent Lion).'

According to Caius, these dogs were often used to fight foxes, badgers, bulls, bears and even lions. 'The force which is in them surmounteth all beleefe, the fast hold which they take with their teeth exceed all credit, three of them against a Bear, force against a Lyon are sufficient, both to try master with them and utterly to out match them.' Caius says Henry VII had these 'bandogges' hung after he pitted them against a lion, maintaining that they had upset the divine right of kings by dispatching the king of the beasts.

One of history's greatest military geniuses, Napoleon Bonaparte, was quick to notice the military efficiency and loyalty of the dog. During the Revolutionary and Napoleonic Wars which ravaged Europe between 1792 and 1815, Napoleon seemed to take on board the words of his hero, Frederick the Great, who famously said: 'The more I see of men, the more I like dogs.' He used a number of dogs in his successful Italian campaign but one called 'Moustache' became famous across Europe.

This unassuming dog saved the day at the start of Napoleon's campaign in Italy. If it had not been for Moustache, Bonaparte could have lost his foray over the Alps and would never have held Europe in his thrall as Emperor. Moustache also has the highly dubious distinction of being the only dog in history to be burned by the Spanish Inquisition. A fabulous and colourful account of this loyal but 'tolerably ugly' dog's remarkable military life was written by Colonel J P Hamilton, published in 1860.

He tells us that this wonder dog was born in Calais in 1799: 'Moustache happened to come upon a parade of Grenadiers. They were brilliantly equipped. Their spirits were high, and their drums loud. Moustache, instantly smitten with their fine appearance, cut the grocer for ever, slunk out of the town and joined the Grenadiers. He was dirty, and tolerably ugly, but there was an intelligence, a sparkle, a brightness about his eye, that could not be overlooked. "We have not a single dog in the regiment', said the petit tambour, 'and at any rate, this one looks clever enough to forage for himself". The drum major assented and Moustache attached himself to the band and was soon found to possess considerable tact and talent.'

Within three weeks, the precocious pup had learned to stand to attention (as best a dog could), go on guard duty and keep time as the troops marched. He accompanied his fellow soldiers in the famous march over Mont St Bernard before sniffing out the enemy as they tried to advance. Col Hamilton writes: 'He gave the alarm and the Austrians rapidly retreated. Next morning, it was decided that Moustache should receive the rations of a Grenadier. He was now cropped *a la militaire*, a collar with the name of the regiment was hung round his neck, and the barber was ordered to comb and shave him once a week.'

Moustache, a cross bred poodle, covered himself in *la gloire* at the Battle of Marengo in 1800 but won eternal fame for his outstanding bravery at one of Napoleon's most famous victories, Austerlitz. According to Colonel Hamilton, Moustache was attached to a unit of light infantry during the momentous battle in 1805. He watched in horror as a fellow French soldier, bearing the colours of his regiment, was surrounded: 'Five or six Austrians still remained by the ensign to obtain possession of the colours he had so nobly defended. Moustache, having thrown himself on the colours, was on the point of being pierced by bayonets, when a timely discharge of grapeshot swept the Austrian into oblivion. He took the staff of the French banner in his teeth and strenuously endeavoured to disengage it, but ineffectually. He succeeded in tearing away the silk and with his glorious trophy returned to the camp, limping and bleeding.'

Despite his valiant conduct at some of the greatest battles in European history, Moustache's remains met a rather ignominious end. A soldier, who didn't recognise Moustache and mistakenly assumed he was a random stray, hit him with the flat edge of his sabre. Our straggly hero took umbrage at being struck, deserted from the regiment and attached himself to a group of heavy cavalry, bound for Spain. In March 1811, he was killed by a cannon ball at the Siege of Badajos. He was buried on the scene of his last glories, collar, medal and all. Col Hamilton says 'A plain stone with the simple *Ci git le brave Moustache* (Here lies the brave Moustache) was placed over his grave but the Spaniards afterwards broke the stone and the bones of the poor animal were burnt by order of the Inquisition.' A sad end for a four legged hero. By the start of the 20th century, however, after being consigned to the military wilderness, dogs were about to enjoy a resurgence.

One man paved the way for the remarkable role of Memphis and his fellow working dogs, namely Lieutenant Colonel Edwin Hautenville Richardson, who worked closely with the world famous Battersea Dogs Home in London. Both Richardson and Battersea have indelibly left their mark on the history of these animals and their rise to prominence within the armed forces.

Anyone interested in the history of military working dogs will sooner or later comes across Richardson. The fact that armed forces around the world now recognise the importance of working dogs is largely down to him. He was a visionary who was years ahead of his time in managing to grasp the utility of dogs in wartime. His campaign to get the military establishment of his time to see how dogs could work on the battlefield was a one man crusade, a labour of love against the prevailing orthodoxy of the early 20th century that wars would be won by artillery and superior firepower alone.

The upper echelons of the Army believed that radio and telegram communications had made the use of dogs as messengers obsolete. Richardson was to prove them wrong. He showed time again that canines offered far more than just service as four legged message carriers.

His achievements were remarkable. He single-handedly established the first British war dog school at the start of the First World War. His books were used as training manuals by the United States' Quartermaster Corps in 1942 when the US started its first official canine army programme. He is also credited with introducing the use of dogs among the British police forces.

Nowadays, Richardson is a rather obscure figure, his achievements and contribution to the nation's war efforts having been somewhat forgotten over the decades. However, among the canine cognoscenti, he is a legendary figure. In most bookshops today it is difficult, if not impossible, to find his works. A cursory glance on Amazon's website reveals that one of his out of print works called *Forty Years with Dogs* is so rare that it is currently changing hands for up to £430 a copy.

In sepia tinted photographs, Lt Col Richardson looks very much a man of the time with his carefully clipped moustache, side parted hair and uniform replete with highly polished buttons, insignia and decorations. His striking eyes, which seem to stare at you intently from the page, convey something of the nature which may be behind his singular success with dogs, a piercing intelligence and a kindness of spirit that would serve him well with his four legged comrades.

Richardson's family had a farming background. He was engrossed with natural history from a young age and attended school in Cheltenham, Gloucestershire, where his passion for animals shone through. His father was keen for him to pick up foreign languages so he was sent to Hanover and Dresden to learn German, a skill that would serve him well in later years. It was while in Europe that he first became fascinated by the history of canines, especially their use in wartime.

Richardson was quick to grasp the growing threat from

Germany. He wrote: 'At that period the Germans were not as sure of themselves as they became later. That they were being tuned up under the stringent educational military propaganda it was to see, but they then were of an admiring frame of mind towards Britishers, and were without that overweening conceit, which later on led them so woefully astray. Even my boyish mind understood, however, that their military organization was not one to hold in light esteem, and that the energy and system which, with true German thoroughness, they introduced into every detail, might be likely to cause us a lot of trouble someday.'

After gaining his officer's commission from Sandhurst, he served in the Sherwood Foresters before joining the West York militia. He married in 1894 and eventually moved to Carnoustie in Angus, Scotland, with his dog loving wife. It was here that his fascination with dogs would develop into a lifelong obsession.

By the outset of the war, the situation in Britain was grim. The country had failed to heed his warnings that dogs could be a 'force multiplier', to use modern military speak. Other powers though, had the foresight to see what dogs could bring to the battlefield. After building up a large kennel of dogs and putting them through their paces, Richardson could get no-one in authority in the British armed forces to listen to his appeals. He said: 'I brought the matter from time to time to the notice of the authorities and although the police supported the idea to a certain extent, especially the forces in provincial towns, who used a number of dogs for patrolling suburban areas, I could get no generally concerted action taken.'

Many other European nations had taken heed of Richardson and started setting up their own dog training schools. While roaming the Scottish countryside, Richardson himself is said to have seen shady German officials buying up hundreds of dogs at the turn of the century. Germany had been experimenting with different dogs in various battlefield roles since the 1870s. The new German Reich had a network of village clubs that bred and trained dogs for military use, years ahead of the British approach at the time. Germany had been buying up British breeds and by August 1914, they had around 6000 dogs ready for service.

In his 1920 book 'British War Dogs: Their training and psychology', Richardson said that Germany at that time had the most organised service of both military and police dogs.

Between 1900 and 1914, he visited Germany's dog training schools. He admired their training methods but believed Britain boasted better breeds that were more suited to this line of work.

'It seemed to me that, as in other forms of German organisation, not enough attention was directed to the psychology of the subject and too much to the letter of mechanical instruction.' In short, Prussian militarism had even infected the German dog training schools.

Despite this canine arms race across the continent, the British Army remained slow to grasp the benefits of four legged soldiers, but Richardson harboured a stubborn streak. Although his warnings falling on deaf ears, he continued to appeal to his superiors on the need for Army dogs.

He said: 'When my offer of sentry dogs was rejected in the first days of the war, I turned to another branch of work in which I had frequently experimented in previous years – tracing the wounded on the battlefield.' As the war deepened, however, conditions on the Western front with lakes of mud, tonnes of barbed wire and infernos of machine gun fire meant there were no opportunities for ambulance dogs.

With a large dose of anti-German sentiment, Richardson tells us: 'When the French Army hurriedly sent some of their ambulance dogs with their keepers to the front in the earliest feverish days, the first thing that happened was that, although both men and dogs wore the Red Cross, the enemy brutally shot them all down whenever they attempted to carry out their humanitarian work. It was also found that when the opposing forces settled down into trench warfare, the opportunities on the Western front were closed. The only ambulance dogs that were used with any success were those with the German army when the Russians were retreating on the Eastern front.'

At the outbreak of war, there were no dogs attached to the British Army with the exception of one Airedale terrier trained by Richardson as a sentry. This remarkable dog vindicated Richardson's repeated calls for the use of dogs on the frontline as he won the highest military accolade, the Victoria Cross. The brave terrier, known as Jack, went from Battersea Dogs Home to the war dog school eventually set up by Richardson in 1916.

Stray Jack was taken from a life of deprivation and squalor on the streets and trained as a sentry and messenger before being shipped over to France. By a quirk of history, he was posted with Richardson's old unit, the Sherwood Foresters. He found himself at a forward post in 1918 just as the Germans made a push, severing all lines of communication with headquarters. Airedale Jack's comrades were in peril, four miles from their headquarters with no way to call for reinforcements. As the merciless German onslaught continued, the men prepared for the final attack and their imminent death.

This was Jack's moment of glory and the action that would win him a VC. His handler, a Lieutenant Hunter, realised Jack was their only hope of salvation. He wrote a note, attached it to the dog's collar and sent Jack on his way. One of the best accounts of Jack's final moments are captured in writer Blythe Hamer's moving celebration of acts of canine courage, *Dogs at War*, and is worth quoting here.

She writes: '"Goodbye Jack, Go back, boy",' said Hunter.

Jack slipped quietly away towards headquarters, staying close to the ground and taking advantage of whatever cover there was, as he had been trained to do. The bombardment was too heavy though and he started to get hit. A piece of shrapnel smashed his jaw, and the battalion watched him stagger on. Another missile ripped open his black and tan coat from shoulder to thigh. Still, he continued forward, using shell craters and trenches for cover. His forepaw was then hit and still Jack dragged himself along the ground on three legs for the last few miles. He persevered until he reached headquarters where he fell dead. He had done a hero's work and saved the battalion.'

The British Imperial War Museum has a memorial marking Jack's sacrifice which reads 'to the memory of Airedale Jack, a hero of the Great War.' Jack's lifesaving actions must have helped to cement Richardson's great love for Airedale terriers. Richardson found that Airedales were perfect for sentry and patrol work due to their strength, intelligence and robust physiques. Wolf and Prince, two other Airedales, would also win Richardson's favour as well as glory on the Western front, helping to convince military chiefs that Britain urgently needed a special military working dog school.

In the winter of 1916, an officer in the Royal Artillery wrote to Richardson requesting dogs to carry messages between batteries and other bases because telephone lines and other forms of communication were often disrupted by artillery barrages that brought down cables and left soldiers buried in the mud, never to be seen again. Plucky Richardson enjoyed a challenge and quickly found the answer. He experimented with hundreds of dogs before he found two that could carry messages over a distance of two miles. The dogs, Wolf and Prince, left for France on the last day of 1916 and went directly to Thiepval under the escort of a gunner.

Reports from Colonel Winter of the Royal Artillery recommended the dogs in glowing terms.

One report says: 'During the operations against Wytschaete Ridge, two messenger dogs attached to this brigade were sent forward at 1.00 am. After being led up to through communication trenches during darkness, they went forward as soon as the attack was launched, passing through the smoke barrage. Both dogs reached brigade headquarters, travelling a distance as the crow flies of 4000 yards over ground they had never seen before and over exceptionally difficult terrain. The dog dispatched at 12.45 pm reached his destination under the hour, bringing in an important message and this was the first message which was received, all visual communication having failed.'

More positive reports on Wolf and Prince followed from frontline commanders, and Richardson attributes the launch of his dog training school in Shoeburyness, Essex, within earshot of the big guns across the Channel, directly to their efforts. Each recruit was tested for three different types of work: messenger, sentry and guard duties. Battersea was the sole source of dogs, making sure that 'many a homeless, deserted stray was saved from the lethal chamber and transformed into a useful member of His Majesty's Forces.'

One of the most famous military dogs of World War One had the unfortunate name of Stubby. He sported a short stubby tail, hence his name, and eventually reached the rank of Sergeant. It is thought that Stubby was an American pit bull terrier, one of the breeds currently outlawed by Britain's controversial Dangerous Dogs Act. He reportedly wandered into a training session at Yale University in Connecticut and caught the eye of Private Robert J Conroy of the US 26th Infantry Division. He quickly won other fans among the soldiers as he could march in step with his comrades, howl along to bugle calls and even manage a salute of sorts by bringing his paw up to his cheek.

In 1917, Conroy sneaked Stubby aboard a troop ship heading

for the killing fields of Europe. Stubby was discovered by a commanding officer but was saved when he snapped off his trademark salute. The gesture warmed the heart of Conroy's superior and he allowed the dog to stay on board. After his arrival on the battlefield, Stubby suffered a gas attack but survived thanks to prompt medical help. He was back at the frontline when another gas attack was launched in the dead of night. Stubby sniffed the deadly chemicals and ran across the sleeping soldiers causing a huge uproar and giving the men time to don their gas masks.

Super Stubby also helped capture a German spy. He often patrolled the battlefield, keeping low and using craters for cover from the hail of enemy fire. He quickly realised that German speaking soldiers were the enemy and English speaking troops were his friends. He would head towards soldiers crying out in English and yelp and bark to attract medics to the wounded men. He would also herd shell-shocked men back to their trenches and their comrades. At one point, a soldier spoke to him in English with a heavy German accent. Stubby stood up straight, growled and charged the man, bringing him to the ground and attacking his legs until help arrived. Stubby's remarkable intuition was proved right, the man was a German agent.

A contemporary account gives the wonderfully colourful story of the tiger striped terrier's extraordinary life: 'Though delighted with his intellectual environment at Yale and his frolics in the huge Bowl, Stubby came to the conclusion that he ought to do his bit by his country. Stubby joined up. One morning a bugle sounded the departure from camp. Crammed into a train loaded with equipment, he was started South.

'On February 5 1918, he entered the front lines of the Chemin des Dames sector, north of Soissons, where he was under fire night and day for more than a month. The noise and strain that shattered the nerves of many of his comrades did not impair Stubby's spirits. Not because he was unconscious of danger. His angry howl while a battle raged and his mad canter from one part of the lines to another indicated realization. But he seemed to know that the greatest service he could render was comfort and cheerfulness. When he deserted the front lines it was to keep a wounded soldier company in the corner of a dugout or in the deserted section of a trench. If the suffering doughboy fell asleep, Stubby stayed awake to watch. In the Chemin des Dames, Stubby captured a German spy and saved a doughboy from a gas attack. Hearing a sound in the stillness of the night, the dog, who guarded sleeplessly, stole out of the trenches and recognized – a German. Attempts by the German to deceive the dog were futile. Seizing his prisoner by the breeches, Stubby held on until help arrived.'

Stubby was injured several times, fought in a total of 17 battles and was the first dog to receive a proper rank from the US Army. He was an international hero and met three presidents, Wilson, Harding and Coolidge. When Stubby died in 1926, he New York Times published a glowing obituary and his body was donated to the world famous Smithsonian museum. Headed 'Stubby of AEF (American Expeditionary Forces) Enters Valhalla', the piece from April 4, 1926 says: 'Stubby is dead. He was only a dog and unpedigreed at that, but he was the most famous mascot in the AEF.'

Stubby was apparently quite a dandy. He wore an embroidered chamois blanket presented to him by admiring Frenchwomen and decorated with service chevrons, medals, pins, buttons and a galaxy of souvenirs. He also sported a German Iron Cross on his bobbed tail which his obituary says 'the possession of which Stubby never explained.'

Dogs provided a vital link between units during many battles at a time when communications were basic and prone to breaking down. Dogs have a lower profile and can move five times faster than a human, making them a difficult target for enemy snipers. During the slaughter of the battle of Verdun in 1916, which caused some 800,000 casualties, 17 men were killed trying to get messages out of one trench line but a brave dog managed to make seven lifesaving runs before he was killed.

One hero messenger dog called Satan won fame at Verdun, also known as France's Stalingrad such was the magnitude of the carnage in this small north eastern corner of the country. Satan became known as the winged dog of Verdun after he ran through withering fire to save his comrades in the French lines. His handler, Duvalle, was waiting for support from the rest of the French Army as supplies of food, water and ammunition dwindled and the Germans relentlessly bombarded their positions.

Their fate looked dismal until Duvalle spotted a black speck on the horizon . It was Satan, a jet black mixed breed dog, dodging and weaving across no-man's land. As Duvalle stood transfixed, thinking that the day may have been saved, Satan crashed to the ground. The dog had been hit by a German bullet. Duvalle stood on the entrenchment and shouted encouragement. He said: '*Courage, Satan, mon ami! Viens pour la France!*' as he too was struck by a fusillade from the German trenches. Satan heard his master's voice, summoned his last reserves of energy and dragged himself the last few hundred yards to the French position. He carried a message telling them to hang on as help was on its way. He also carried a basket containing carrier pigeons. They were sent back with an urgent message to destroy a German battery. One pigeon made it through the hail of bullets, the battery was silenced and the French held on to a strategically vital part of Verdun.

Military working dogs served their respective countries well during the Great War but like their human comrades in arms, suffered horrific casualties. A 1917 issue of Animals magazine estimates that 7000 dogs were killed during World War One but as author Blythe Hamer points out, this figure is likely to be far too low. Many countries used military dogs so the death toll could easily be ten times higher. It is also very difficult to calculate how many humans owed their lives to these dogs. There can be no doubt that large numbers of troops were saved by these canine heroes.

Sadly, army chiefs did not take on board the lessons of the Great War and the numerous accounts of canine courage under fire. The French euthanised all 15,000 dogs in their *Service des Chiens de Guerre* unit once the war ended. Many dogs that served in the British, German, Italian and Russian military were also put down.

Lt Col Richardson watched in anguish as Britain let its canine army fall apart. The British top brass in World War Two was convinced that mechanisation and modernisation would win the war. There was no place for the dogs of the last war. Despite sterling efforts by Richardson to convince the War Office otherwise, it would be 1942 before the government set up the Army War Dog School.

Maria Dickin, founder of the Peoples Dispensary for Sick Animals (PDSA), was so impressed by the work of dogs and animals in the war effort, she introduced a special medal dubbed the animals' Victoria Cross to mark their sacrifice. A total of eleven dogs won the medal, a bronze medallion bearing the words 'For Gallantry' and 'We Also Serve', during the war.

The first recipient was a mongrel called Bob who served with the 6th Royal West Kent Regiment. Bob received the award on 24 March 1944 for saving the lives of many men as he worked on patrols in Green Hill, Tunisia. He stopped his patrol sharply as they approached the enemy lines at night. The soldiers tried to push on but Bob stood his ground and wouldn't let them progress any further. The enemy were actually far closer than their intelligence sources had told them, and so Bob saved his comrades from certain death. An Alsatian called Rifleman Khan also won the medal after he saved a Lance Corporal Muldoon who nearly drowned during heavy shell fire at the assault on Walcheren, in the Netherlands in November 1944, while serving with the Cameronians (Scottish Rifles).

The ancestors of the IED busting dogs of today's Afghanistan conflict came to the fore during World War Two. Mine dogs were trained to sit down when they located the scent of a device. Dogs were far more effective than metal detectors and were able to pick up mines made of different materials such as glass, plastic and wood. In Russia, one legendary mine detecting dog called Zucha unearthed 2000 mines in just 18 days.

The Soviets did learn from their experiences with working dogs in World War Two. They would use them to great effect in their otherwise disastrous invasion and occupation of Afghanistan from 1979 to 1989. The Islamic Mujahideen fighters used thousands of mines to defend their bases and storage sites. Military expert Scott McMichaels says that in 1987 alone, Soviet engineers disarmed or destroyed 4882 anti-tank mines, 3800 anti-personnel mines and 1162 fougasse, a form of improvised mine made of a hollow in the ground filled with high explosives and projectiles to cause maximum casualties among unsuspecting troops.

To counter the huge threat from mines, the Soviets used mobile engineer detachments with tracked vehicles, tanks with mine rollers and detection dogs. McMichaels says: 'This was hard, nerve wracking work. Soviet studies show that the effectiveness of dismounted engineers performing this function in the heat dropped to 50 percent after one and a half to two hours and to 20 to 25 percent after three hours.'

One dog was lauded for its performance despite only discovering the relatively small numbers of ten mines and two fougasses in two years. British dogs today in Afghanistan may find scores of IEDs in just one six month tour. One bitter conflict, more than any other campaign, deeply shaped the tactics and techniques of British Army dogs like Memphis, Benji, Kevin and Molly working in Afghanistan. That was the campaign in Northern Ireland, euphemistically known as 'The Troubles'.

As the province slid into anarchy and effectively civil war, the Provisional Irish Republican Army vowed to oust the British Army from Northern Ireland and unite the six counties of the north with the Republic of Ireland in the south. Their tactic was the roadside bomb, or what came to be known in more recent times as the IED. According to the Army's own history, growing unrest in Northern Ireland in April 1969 led to the creation of a highly specialised dog unit. Five Army dog handlers would lose their lives during Operation Banner, the military codename for its mission in Northern Ireland from 1969 to 2007.

Personnel from the Royal Army Veterinary Corps (RAVC) Training Centre and the RAVC Tactical Dog Troop at Aldershot were sent to provide guard dogs to provide security at the infamous Long Kesh camp which came to be known by various names: The H Blocks, The Maze or just simply Maze prison. As open civil war threatened to engulf the whole of Northern Ireland, army chiefs realised that protection and specialist dogs were vital in the war against terrorists on both sides of the sectarian divide.

Demand for trained handlers rapidly outstripped the RAVC's supply. On May 1 1973 the Army Dog Unit (ADU) was formed. Within a year, around 180 men from over 60 different regiments and corps were serving with the unit. Without doubt, their work combating the IRA's teams of expert bomb makers paved the way for the doggy heroes of Afghanistan. The unit's dogs and handlers were second to none, becoming experts in three disciplines, just as dog handlers do today.

61

ADU handlers used guard or attack dogs known as 'Snappers or Land Sharks' to the troops. They also deployed, with Arms Explosive Search (AES), dogs known as 'Wagtails' or tracker dogs affectionately called 'Groundhogs'. The dogs were incredibly effective against the worst that Loyalist and Republican death squads could throw at them.

Northern Ireland veteran and former dog handler Dave Harding was on the frontline with the unit for 14 years. The 44-year-old Mancunian still suffers from Post-Traumatic Stress Disorder (PTSD) after witnessing unspeakable carnage on the streets of the province between 1983 and 1997. Dave, a former Rifleman with the Royal Green Jackets, served across the province helping to counter the IRA's bombing campaign. The Provo's bloody onslaught would claim hundreds of lives.

First Dave had to overcome his deep fear of dogs. In his broad Manchester accent, Dave described to me his unlikely foray into the world of military canines. A childhood brush with a bad tempered dog led to a long phobia. Desperate for a change to his army career, he applied to do a dog handling course hoping to revitalise his work life and end, once and for all, his fear of dogs.

He said: 'I loved it. After walking into kennels for the first time, in 30 seconds, my fear was gone forever. Working with dogs is unbelievable, the bond that builds is totally beyond belief.' Dave now runs an association for serving and retired handlers. He said the extreme conditions faced by dog handlers in Afghanistan shared many similarities with the Northern Ireland conflict. There was one major difference though, the war in Afghanistan was far more intense.

He said: 'The boys and girls in Afghanistan have our highest respect. Every member of the unit says the same, the intensity, the amount of finds they are having to deal with, it's unbelievable compared to our day. They really do a great job.' The Taliban and the IRA use similar 'shoot and scoot' tactics, according to Dave. He said: 'The IRA bomb makers are just as good as the Taliban bomb makers. They are using liquid based bombs now while the IRA relied on Semtex. The Taliban have been boiling down fertiliser, adding oil or whatever to it and there you go. There's your explosive. They are using the same basics: to lay a bomb, you have to think sick. You have to think 'where can I get these people?' It's a second guess game. The Taliban put out a main bomb, but possibly leave a second because they know if a British soldier is injured, his mates will go and get him out. They are all singing from the same hymn book and using fairly similar techniques. That's why the military working dog units do such a tremendous job out there.'

The Northern Ireland experience of outwitting the bombers would prove invaluable in Afghanistan. Devious IRA chiefs even used innocuous looking camera flash guns to trigger bombs. Dave had witnessed IRA bombers use a chain of flashes, each triggering the next with the last flash triggering a bomb. Dave explained that handlers, working at the limits of human endurance, and their dogs form such a close bond under the extreme stresses of combat that the connection resembles the warmth and devotion of a parent and child relationship.

The dogs were like children, often needing their 'daddy' to keep them in line: 'If Sam misbehaved, I would make a big 'no' noise and point at him to say, 'Daddy isn't happy with you'. Some lads would get a hold of their dog's harness and give it a shake. Once you took the collar off and put the issue harness on, that was the signal to the dog 'right, you are going to work now'.'

During one of his tours of duty, Dave suffered every soldier's worst nightmare when he was blown up carrying out his duties in the toughest part of Belfast. The most difficult moment of his army career came on January 24th 1994 when he had to go back to the same location. He said: 'The night before, we had closed the barriers after we searched them. It was very high risk because we were there twice that day. Just after closing the barrier, a coffee jar device came over and landed three metres away from me.' The coffee jar bomb was the IRA's infamous improvised hand grenade. The coffee jar was packed with semtex and primed to explode. A crude but effective release system inside the jar would have been wired up so that when the glass broke, two metal prongs would meet and form a circuit, detonating the bomb. Dave was thrown from his feet. As he clambered upright again, his ears rang from the blast. It had been so loud that it almost perforated his eardrums. For hours, he had to stay in position, disorientated and suffering shock. The next morning, he had to return to the blast site. Thanks to these horrific experiences and others, he now suffers from Post-Traumatic Stress Disorder.

He said: 'I was doing searches with my knees literally knocking together because you know there is something there. At certain times you just need that little bit extra to say right let's get going. The dogs loved it, it was one big game. It sounds stupid but you should have seen the dogs' faces. They were enjoying themselves, smiling.'

Dave and his buddy Sam worked together very successfully as a search team but they went their separate ways when Dave's tour finished. Dave worked with Sam for more than two years and had to give him up just after the dog's fourth birthday. 'He was my dog, he wasn't an instrument just to be used for searching for six months before being passed on to another soldier. He was my dog until my tour was up or my regiment said I couldn't get more extensions to my time. We did a two year tour then we could apply for an extension. It is a job you could never explain. The satisfaction is unbelievable. Any other job I did in the army was peanuts compared to working with dogs.'

He was to meet Sam once more but sadly the reunion was not a happy one. Dave was training troops in Germany, tramping across the hillside with a gaggle of new recruits. By a strange coincidence, Sam was working in Germany at the time. He saw Dave in the distance and, ignoring his new handler, galloped down the hill to welcome his old pal. In a flurry of drool and paws, Sam scrambled all over Dave. This well-meaning display meant he had broken a golden rule by disregarding his new 'daddy'. Dave said: 'I had never hit a dog and I had to just give him a wee slap on the snout and tell him to go away. If I hadn't done it, then his handler wouldn't have been able to handle him. When I hit him, I nearly burst out crying. It remains the most horrible thing I had to do but I knew his new handler was a great bloke and I knew he was going to be in good hands. Sometime later, I was speaking to another soldier and he was describing working with a military working dog. It turned out it was my Sam. He had been working brilliantly just as he had done with me. That meant a lot. It really made my day.'

Over time, the Army Dog Unit (Northern Ireland) would eventually evolve into today's 1st Military Working Dog Regiment. The special role played by the unit was recognised in 1974 when personnel were granted the right to wear a red paw badge in their headdress next to their regimental cap badge. The badge, the smallest semi-official emblem in the Army, represents the bloody paws of dogs that had to carry out their duties while walking over broken glass.

This badge of honour was worn by handlers with pride for years. In time, a tactical recognition flash or insignia was worn on the left shoulder of their combat uniform, setting them apart from other soldiers on duty.

In 2009, as I was preparing to go to Afghanistan, members of Dave's association gathered at the National Arboretum in Staffordshire. They unveiled a striking plaque to five Army dog handlers and their dogs that were killed serving in Northern Ireland. The jet black stone proudly sports two bright red paws in recognition of their highly specialised unit. The memorial, which sits on top of a large grey granite slab, also features the picture of the two dogs killed in action: German Shepherd Oliver and black Labrador Ben. These loyal, brave dogs of war did not die in vain since the techniques they pioneered are being used to this day in Helmand.

SIX

The Most Important Toy in the World

Memphis looks like a cute family pet, but working dogs and their handlers form a military elite and few are tough enough to make the grade. It's unbelievable to think that these dogs risk everything for the sake of a toy. Saving lives for them is, literally, one big game.

The relentless pace of operations in Afghanistan means that the demand for canine combatants and handlers is higher than at any time since World War Two. Army chiefs, however, have not lowered their standards to turn more raw recruits into teams. It is clear that dog teams have to be on top of their game to make the grade in today's Army. Unlikely as it may sound, thousands of our soldiers' and marines' lives depend on the most innocuous of objects – a chewed tennis ball, a frayed dolly or even, in some cases, a rolled up pair of socks, toys that provide the motivation the dogs need to sniff out IEDs, day in and day out, in Afghanistan.

The rigorous selection process for would-be dog soldiers is harder now than it has ever been. Dog handlers are, first and foremost, soldiers. Memphis and Mick endured months of arduous physical training before being allowed to hit the ground in Afghanistan. Army recruiters have gone a long way to dispel the notion that today's youngsters are a generation of junk food eating, computer game addicts, taking young recruits and turning them into warriors fit to fight in the toughest terrain imaginable.

Candidates have to undergo a robust selection process before they are even allowed to join the Army. Aspirant soldiers first take a touch screen computer exercise called the British Army Recruit Battery test. The 30 minute ordeal is designed to assess their mental dexterity and the speed of reaction. Once they have passed this test, and a series of interviews, they are packed off to a two day stay at any one of a number of Army selection centres around the country. Recruiters examine their fitness, confidence, teamwork skills and basic knowledge of the Army. Candidates are also put through a military medical, an ordeal sure to send a shiver down a young recruit's spine.

In time honoured tradition a doctor will tell them to remove their undergarments, cup their private parts and cough. They then have to lift a weight to a height of 1.45 metres, simulating the lifting of heavy ammunition and supply boxes onto the back of Army trucks. Next test is the jerry-can challenge, where candidates have to carry two 20 kg water containers over a set course of more than 100 metres in under two minutes. Physical training instructors then line up the recruits for a 1.5 mile run which must be completed in less than 14 minutes.

The Army's fitness guide boasts, 'The British Army is the fittest in the world, employing tried and tested training programmes that are guaranteed to build levels of stamina, strength and stability'.

Trainee soldiers are left in no doubt about the importance of all round fitness from the start of their careers, and applicants are encouraged to start training even before they cross the threshold of the recruitment office.

The British Army has long been a pioneer in developing fitness plans. More than 150 years ago, after the bloodshed of the Crimean War, it set about building the first 'Army Gymnastic Staff'. The benefits of the training it offered, which included boxing, fencing, gymnastics, and general physical activity, were soon apparent and, by 1862, it was decided that there should be a gym in every garrison with its own officer and instructional staff.

The Army's fitness bible says: 'Physical Training Instructors, while keeping abreast of the latest sport science developments, have stayed true to the fundamentals of exercise proven to be effective through the ages.' So, forced marches in all-weathers, up and down gut busting hills, are still the order of the day for any prospective dog soldier. Extreme sleep deprivation and intense physical exercise remain the lot of soldiers to this day, exactly as they were in years gone by.

Civilians are often shocked by the physical and mental robustness required for aspiring soldiers. Indeed, despite the best efforts of recruiters, it often comes as a surprise to many ill prepared would-be troopers. However, these tests pale beside the challenges faced by pups as they begin their path towards becoming military working dogs. Successful search dogs such as Memphis must be at the peak of their physical and psychological fitness with a powerful instinct to play and search. These two canine instincts are intrinsically linked. Army selectors look for dogs that are brave, loyal, possessive, and eager to please but, above all, playful. From the first day of training dogs, whether explosives search or drug detection dogs, must maintain a consistently high standard, and off days must be few and far between.

The US military trains its elite dog teams at Lackland Air Force Base in Texas. To keep progressing through 'dog school', drug detector dogs must have a 90 per cent success rate, rising to 95 per cent for explosives search dogs for obvious reasons – they are seeking out a far deadlier target. If any team fails to meet this rate for three consecutive training events, they will be kicked off the course and have to retrain from scratch.

Similar stringent standards are enforced across the British

military. The Defence Animal Centre in Melton Mowbray, Leicestershire, is Britain's hub for war dogs. Four legged soldiers are put through their paces here before being deployed around the UK, Afghanistan or anywhere that British forces are based. After a dog arrives at the centre, it will have a week to settle into the kennels before being checked by a vet and given a hip X-ray to make sure it is fighting fit.

Training then begins in earnest. Recruiters know that dogs, like humans, are individuals and can react differently to strange environments. Some animals may be bold while others are skittish and reluctant to meet strangers. So, the first test: dogs are assessed on how they react to different terrain. Assessors want to see that the prospective detection dog can perform the same tasks in a strange environment as in a comfortable, domestic location.

A dog's drive to get its ball is tested outdoors. The ball is thrown into grass or scrub so the dog can't see it although it will know roughly where it landed. The dog is then commanded to 'seek on'. At this stage, it is not essential that the dog finds the ball. Military staff are just keen to make sure that the dog is highly driven and continues to search without signs of distraction or boredom. A good dog will search for ten minutes although five minutes is quite acceptable to the trainers. The dog is then taken indoors and allowed to roam freely, whilst being closely observed on how it reacts to slippery floors, obstacles, and dark, unfamiliar rooms.

Sense of smell is fundamental to an arms and explosive, or drug detection, dog. A four legged recruit is first introduced to the explosive TNT, or Trinitrotoluene. Handlers and trainers have found that it is the most difficult substance for dogs to find. If Rover can find TNT, he can find anything. An officer rolls a ball on to a container holding TNT while watching the doggy recruit intently. The container has small holes through which the scent escapes. When confronted with a new surprising scent, a dog can react in a number of ways. It may stop, wag its tail or twitch its head. The ball is thrown on the source of the unusual smell and positive reinforcement is applied with loads of shouts of 'Good girl!' and 'Well done!' For the dog, the smell is the miracle pathway to its beloved toy. It finds the scent and – hey presto! – its favourite toy 'appears'.

This military twist on the famous Pavlovian reaction is effective. Russian psychologist Pavlov lent his name to this process also known as the 'conditioned reflex'. His experiments in the early 1900s showed that dogs could be conditioned to respond automatically to external stimuli. In a series of famous tests, he presented food to dogs at the same time as a bell rang. The dogs eventually came to associate the ringing of the bell with the presentation of the food and salivated purely upon hearing the bell. In short, through a period of encouragement and reinforcement, dogs are trained to associate certain smells with rewards. The whole process is repeated from start to finish until the dog is happy and confident with the system.

Detection and guard dogs must pass certain tests which are a straight pass or fail. These include accepting a muzzle, and getting in and out of a white dog van without hesitation. They must also get used to hearing weapons ear-splittingly close as they are fired from just 50, or even 25, metres away. Any tantrums or panicking and they have failed. Detection dogs have to show the ability to retrieve a ball indoors and outdoors, while a guard dog must also be able to search and find a ball or other object in an immediate, or delayed, blind retrieve, which means without having been shown it, or smelling it, first.

More importantly for guard dogs, also known as protection dogs, their bite must be worse than their bark. It may not live up to their macho aggressive image but guard dogs are first given a dolly to test their ability to bite and hold, crucial for bringing down any bad guys. The dog then moves onto a bite pad which gives it more confidence to bite closer to the training

71

assistant's body. Once the dog can manage three consecutive sustained bite and holds on the hard sleeve it is introduced to a moving target. Again, three consecutive sustained bite and holds must be achieved.

Guard or protection dogs are trained in an environment designed to closely match the area they are intended to work in, whether they are providing force protection at Air Force bases or guarding the perimeter wire at a nuclear naval base. Teams are trained at all hours of the day and night as they could be expected to operate at any time once they are deemed operational. The dogs have to be able to pick up a scent, be fearless and aggressive and have a good bite (a bad bite if you happen to be on the receiving end).

In addition, military working dogs can be either single or dual purpose. Search dogs are single purpose animals, they either hunt for arms and explosives, or drugs, never both. If a dog was to search for drugs AND bombs, when he alerted to a substance the handler would have to figure out whether it was a stash of herbal cannabis or a 300 kilogramme IED, primed and ready to explode.

Some canines are dual trained so that they can carry out more than one task, such as patrolling and drug detection. German Shepherds, Belgian Malinois and Dutch Shepherds are the order of the day for this work. Patrol dogs are required to check and clear buildings, patrol parking areas, housing blocks, and troop bases, so they have to get used to a broad range of environments.

According to a dog handler manual, patrol/guard dogs are highly effective for a huge range of jobs including: anti-terrorism; force protection; Military Police investigations; walking and mobile patrols; alarm responses; building searches; apprehension of individuals; civil disturbances; and guarding high risk targets. One handler, said: 'These types of dog are similar to police dogs. They are trained to protect with or without a command from handler. The dogs are trained to assess the threat and act accordingly. These are definitely not the average family pooch. They will go for certain sensitive areas on a target and take them down without a second thought.'

Families hoping to donate their dog to the military can rest easy, knowing that their beloved pooch will be very well looked after. Defence chiefs make five promises to anyone considering donating or selling their dog to the military. The MoD website says: 'Be assured that your dog will be cared for, stimulated and trained through positive reward based training, *ie* plenty of ball work, play and focused games.' the Defence Animal Centre pledges to give the dogs what they call 'The Five Freedoms'. These are: Freedom from Hunger; Freedom from Pain, Injury and Disease; Freedom from Fear and Distress; Freedom from Physical Discomfort and Freedom to perform most normal forms of behaviour.

No good soldier's training would be complete without an assault course, or the doggy equivalent. Dogs are exposed to a series of obstacles that will be familiar to anyone who has seen Crufts or a police dog display team in action. Various obstacles are used to simulate walls, open windows, tunnels, ramps and steps. Dogs learn to negotiate their way around these courses. It also gives the handlers a chance to form a bond with their dogs and ensures the canine soldier is not bewildered by similar environments in a real operational scenario.

World renowned dog behaviour expert Stuart Kemp served 24 years with the British Army's dogs. A former regimental sergeant major in the Royal Logistic Corps, he saw action leading dog teams on the front-line in Afghanistan, the Gulf War, Bosnia and Kosovo. The Welshman, who now runs the Blue Ridge Canine Academy, said the bonds formed in training between a soldier and their dog lasts a lifetime.

He said: 'Unfortunately, death is a fact of life in this business.

One dog going across a suspected minefield does save hundreds of soldiers' lives, but occasionally things go wrong. When you have been partners with a dog for an average of four to five years, it cuts deep. It is a necessary evil; and that's not something that everyone will want to hear. It is a fact of life. They are animals but very much part of the family once the work shift is over.'

A dog's breed was considered important during training but a lot comes down to the individual canine's psychology, according to Kemp. During the training process, an old chewed up tennis ball takes on a huge amount of significance. Sporting a t-shirt with the logo 'You are the leader, your dog is the follower', Stuart retains an unmistakable martial air. His dark utility clothing, short clipped hair and black shades add to his no-nonsense demeanour. Stuart though, is a real softy at heart, even getting down on all fours to help young children deal with an errant family pooch.

He explained about Army dog training, telling me: 'Whether a guard dog, guard attack dog, or a sniffer dog for drugs, Semtex, or IEDs, it's all based on positive reinforcement training. Your Spaniels and Labs and Collies who do the search and rescue will pretty much do anything for a ball. That ball could be 99p from a local supermarket but with a dog, from the beginning of your relationship, you guard that ball with your life. That ball goes with you everywhere. The dog sees whatever its doing as a game. That's the idea generally, if you can get a dog to do something that pleases it as a game and it gets a reward afterwards, you are 75 per cent of the way there.'

Keeping the job fun is a key task for any good handler, and holding the dogs interest is a theme that unites handlers around the world and across the decades, working with German Shepherds in Bosnia, trained to attack and arrest intruders, or dogs deployed in Northern Ireland in the early 80s, all the way through to today's dogs teams in Afghanistan. Stuart said:

'The first thing that has to be ascertained is whether or not that dog is suitable for the role you are looking at. There are some Spaniels out there who would be better off as guard attack dogs and some German Shepherds who are better at search and rescue or bomb detection.'

Different breeds are associated with certain traits but a lot depends on the animal's individuality and personality. A dog is tested on how it reacts to going through water, dealing with heights and facing raging fires. Stuart added: 'The dog's intelligence is tested with exercises, the agility of the dog is tested, mental stability of the dog is assessed and obviously the medical state of the dog is constantly assessed by medical professionals. That happens twice to three times a year.'

With the rigours of combat in mind, every effort is made to make sure that the dog can function while hearing loud noises. In Afghanistan, a dog team could be within earshot of a chilling array of deadly and incredibly loud weaponry, from mortars to Javelin missiles to 50 calibre heavy machine guns. 'Dogs are not allowed to become noise sensitive. If they do, they would not be any good, certainly on the explosive ordnance disposal side of life. There is no massively scientific way this is done. Children's cap guns, starter pistols, moving on to shotguns could be used. Each time, the dog is rewarded for the behaviour you want, which is to remain steady. They get rewarded with food and a toy. Sometimes a dog will be really steady, even on a C4 explosion, but if a dog is unsteady it's considered for other roles. Just because it is noise sensitive doesn't mean it won't make a good nose dog. You do spend a lot of time training these dogs so the last thing you want to do is give them up at the last hurdle. If they didn't love the job, they simply wouldn't do it.'

Stuart is married to his 'long suffering wife of 22 years', Toni, and shares his home with his daughter Charlie, a black Labrador called George and a black German Shepherd called Shaka. He explained that dogs that do not make the grade as a front-line working dog are considered for other less challenging roles. If nothing suitable can be found, then they are re-homed.

During our chat, Stuart let me into a secret in the military dog world, one which was confirmed by other military sources. In Afghanistan, it is not unheard of for soldiers to take local strays under their wing and train them for combat. He told me: 'It's not just dogs that are trained back in Blighty and then shipped forward into theatre. There are several occasions when you would find strays near a base and they become mascots. Some of those are trained up because they know the area. Local knowledge is priceless and they will take you a lot of the safe routes, believe it or not. It's something that people don't know about. You don't really hear about but it still goes on. It's hush-hush because when it comes to time to get the dogs back to the UK, a lot of times it is not allowed. You do get some successful cases.'

Stuart has put his years on the front-line to good use and now works in the fight against terrorism, drugs and human trafficking with dog units from some of the world's finest police and security services. Above all, training is a way of forming an unbreakable bond between dog and handler. According to Stuart, many handlers would gladly lay down their life for their four legged comrade in arms. He said: 'Let's say you are a young Lance Corporal in a section, second in command of a unit of eight men. You are responsible for eight guys plus yourself. It's no different when you are a dog handler and you have a dog. Ultimately, the relationship you build between yourself and your companion is unlike anything else. You would die for him as much as he would die for you. That's not how it's meant to be in all the training manuals, but you can ask any handler and that would be the case out there in Afghanistan if push came to shove.'

For dog handlers, their canine charge becomes a fellow

soldier. You look after your dog as best you can, even if it means sticking him in your Bergen backpack. For Stuart, the bond between a dog and his handler is hard to explain to someone who hasn't experienced it: '. . . unless you have a dog living with you 24 hours a day, seven days a week, facing life and death and sharing the same hardships, a dog you have personally trained for all of its life and which has become your sole responsibility. I am a family man as well, so I have kids – but it's a different relationship. It guts you losing a dog in combat, the same way it does when you lose one of your blokes. If I was ever asked to euthanise a dog other than for medical reasons, I would be testing my patience as to whether I would turn that around. Fortunately I have never been asked to make that decision or been asked to carry it out.'

The Defence Animal Centre reassures families that they will find a home for a dog even if they do not make it through training. Army chiefs say that unsuitable dogs will be returned to their owner or they will find them a loving home from a database of eligible families. Once a dog finishes training, it may be employed with the Army, Royal Air Force, Royal Navy, Military Provost Guard Service, Ministry Of Defence Police or Military Guard Service either in the UK or abroad in 'potentially lifesaving operations'.

Some working dogs however, could sadly never be re-homed. Stuart told me that while he was in Kosovo, he trained guard attack dogs to bring an assailant down as quickly as possible. 'Dogs are trained with dual handlers so that they can easily work with two handlers and then work around the clock if needs be. It is very rare to adopt these kind of military work-ing dogs; unlike say, police dogs. These dogs are trained in a different way from the search dogs. Some dogs will actually grab your face and do whatever is required to take down an assailant. So clearly those kind of dogs can never be suitable for re-homing.'

Stuart explained that when dogs like this are retired, some will be given a new lease of life in the form of a specialised training role to help develop other dog teams. Sometimes, however, these dogs have to be humanely euthanised by the veterinary corps. Stuart added: 'That's the way it is. But certain breeds are re-homed including German Shepherds. At the end of their careers, the breeds such as Collies and Spaniels do often get allowed to stay with their handlers.'

It's reassuring to find that some dogs are lucky enough to give up their life or death 'game' in Afghanistan by retiring to enjoy a home fit for a hero back in the UK. For most military working dogs though, a life of lying on the living room couch is still many years away.

SEVEN

The dragon bites back

Mick and Memphis have been apart for weeks. The normally stoic, former shipyard worker gets distinctly dewy eyed, pausing often to clear his throat as he speaks to me from a ward at the Defence Medical Rehabilitation Centre at Headley Court in Surrey. His words reveal just how much he loves and misses his partner.

He hasn't seen him since the day of the IED blast. It is clear from what he says that working with these incredible animals is far more than job, it is a vocation, a calling. For Mick and guys like him, working with dogs on the front-line is unlike any other role in the British military.

He tells me how some handlers even take Christmas presents to their canine comrades before they give gifts to members of their own family. Dogs are an unwavering pal for many people, always there with a wag of the tail to raise their spirits. To Mick, his dog is much more than that. He makes it clear that the remarkable connection between man and animal, forged in the extreme stress of combat, goes far beyond mere companionship. A handler such as Mick is 'daddy' while his dog is his 'boy' or his 'girl'. This closeness between dog and handler is truly unique in the military.

Technically, dogs are classed as equipment. In strictly utilitarian terms, they are a means to an end, another tool used to defeat the Taliban's most feared weapon, the IED. In reality, dogs are much more than a mere tool. Mick is a highly trained handler with the RAF Police, although his role means that he has served side by side with Britain's best known, elite frontline units. RAF Police dogs often get overlooked in favour of their Army counterparts but they provide an essential 'force protection component to military operations worldwide', according to the Ministry of Defence.

Since World War Two, these dog teams have been used to guard RAF airfields and military assets, recover evidence, maintain public order, detect drugs and smash terrorist cells. As Mick's experience shows, they are also deployed on operations in every part of the world, from Singapore, Aden, Hong Kong, Northern Ireland, the Falkland Islands, Bosnia, Kosovo, Gibraltar, Cyprus, Kuwait, Saudi Arabia, to Iraq and Afghanistan.

From Clydebank, near Glasgow, Mick gave up a promising career in the world famous shipyards of the River Clyde to take up his dog handler vocation with the RAF Police. After his spell working in the famous John Brown shipyards, he joined the RAF police in March 1997. He was to go a long way from the grime and decay of post-industrial Scotland to the heat and danger of Helmand Province.

After joining the RAF, he completed normal basic training and police training before volunteering to become a dog handler. He said: 'We all go down to the Defence Animal Centre at Melton Mowbray for training. At Melton, most people are Army personnel, but you will find that the majority of team leaders and section heads are RAF Police. 'I became a drug dog handler in Diego Garcia in the Indian Ocean with the Royal Navy. I was stationed out there for 14 months, then I came back and got an office job in counter intelligence.'

He also completed tours of duty in Iraq and twice in the Falklands. In Iraq, he was a patrol dog handler so he and his dog were deployed by helicopter wherever they were needed. At night, he and his charge would provide security for British bases. Mortar and rocket attacks were a constant danger – he would often hit the dirt not knowing whether his next breath was to be his last. 'It was quite hairy. If there was anything of value, we would guard it.'

He struggled to get his dream deployment to Afghanistan, pestering his bosses for years to get a chance to test his mettle on front-line operations. His dedication paid off and he was eventually deployed as an arms and explosive search dog handler when demand increased for search dogs in the Afghan badlands.

Mick, with the hairs standing on the back of his neck, relived the fateful moments when he 'chased the dragon' with sidekick Memphis on their last mission. Considering the nerve shredding stress of facing death at every step, he could be forgiven for having second thoughts about his sudden career change.

It was August 2011 and Springer Spaniel Memphis looked every inch the professional as he scoured the terrain with his head down and tail bobbling in the air. Every day, the inseparable duo would spearhead patrols with the Royal Marine Commandos. Mick was well behind Memphis crossing some open ground between compounds when the massive IED exploded.

He told me: 'If Memphis had been closer at the time, it might not have happened. There was a flash of light and then a dust cloud and the Marine beside me jumped on top of me, saying: 'Mick, you're OK. Everything's still there.''

Despite his horrendous injuries, Mick was actually lucky, he is one of the few people to have survived a major IED strike. He lived because the bomb only partially detonated.

His horrific ordeal near Checkpoint Toki was captured on camera by documentary filmmaker Chris Terrill. Chris spent six months with Mick and 42 Commando in Helmand province. His work was shown on Channel 5 in the series *Royal Marines: Mission Afghanistan.*

Mick relived the minutes before he nearly died: 'I was there for about a month, brought back in to recalibrate; meaning I was there to get the dog's nose switched on by giving him a series of tests to make sure he was still working properly. I went on rest and recuperation and then back out to Toki. It was on my second patrol that I was injured. We were patrolling to a target compound in the morning, about 200 yards from our checkpoint. I had Memphis off the lead because I was putting him left and right into different areas to search ahead of us.'

Their patrol was approaching a VP or Vulnerable Point, a likely spot where the Taliban would place IEDs to cause maximum casualties. He planned to call Memphis back so he could search up to the vulnerable point, but the Taliban had placed the bomb further out than normal. Mick stepped on the pressure plate, triggering the device.

He said: 'Fortunately for me, it was only a partial detonation. The lads tell me it was about twenty kilogrammes of explosive, so if it had all gone off I wouldn't be here. I have counted my lucky stars every day from then to now and dare say I will be doing that for years.

'My left heel has been shattered and I have got multiple fractures to my left foot. They cut my trousers off to look for any major bleeds and to make sure there was nothing that they had missed. I had burns and shrapnel on my right leg but I was quite lucky since I was wearing bomb proof pants for underwear. There was a huge flash of light when it happened. Then there was a big dust cloud. After the marine checked me for injuries, at that point, I calmed down as he said I had all my limbs, all my bits. I told them it was my left ankle that was hurt so they started strapping it together.'

Mick relieves the pressure with a laugh as he confesses that he was actually happy not to endure the daily dance with death at Toki. 'The whole time, I was near the end of my tour and thinking: thank God, I don't have to walk around here for the next month as. I knew I would be going home. One of the lads came and took Memphis away because he just didn't know what was happening. I think he was just wondering what was going on. Someone else had taken hold of him but I think that threw him and he was wondering why someone else was touching him when I was there.'

Memphis was bemused and frightened by the frantic activity, the shouts and screams, the dust and chaos. He was taken to safety by another marine, all the time wondering what had happened to his 'daddy'. Mick said: 'With everyone shouting instructions and stuff, it was all a bit confusing for him. I was in agony once they tied my feet together to drag me out of the blast area. Then the Royal Navy medic with us gave me morphine. That calmed me down. I think from the initial blast to me being on the emergency helicopter was about 14 minutes. As soon as you get on that helicopter they start giving you painkillers and checking, sorting you out. From there it was straight back to Camp Bastion.'

As the 37-year-old chatted about his horrific experiences, it was apparent that he is far from the public's image of the stereotypical squaddie. He is older, more articulate and less musclebound than the popular image of a soldier. Pictures of him in Afghanistan shortly before his brush with death show a slim, mousey haired man who looks more like a white collar professional than a seasoned combat veteran.

Undoubtedly, Mick's high level of fitness enabled his body to cope with the trauma. The rigours of combat infantry training sessions had prepared him well for the physical battles ahead. He had been shocked by the physical demands when he arrived in Sennelager, Germany in November 2010 to start training with 103 Military Working Dog Squadron.

'We were given one day to settle, then things began in earnest.

The shock to the system came from the amount of physical training that we had to take. This wasn't a 'let's go for a gentle jog round the airfield', it was 'let's sprint in boots until you are sick or near collapse'. It was a rude awakening to most of the RAF handlers. Personally I found it very difficult to keep up with the pace. We persevered and it became easier in time, with all of our handlers completing RAF and Army personal fitness tests. Not one of the RAF handlers dropped out, however it wasn't a hundred percent pass for everyone. I didn't realize at the time but I would be extremely grateful to the physical training instructors for pushing me and getting me prepared for the rigours of tabbing (marching at speed) across Helmand.'

Mick remembers the moment that changed the path of his life when he was given his licence to work with Memphis at exactly 05.00 hrs on March 24. Just two hours later, he was on a Royal Navy Sea King heading for Checkpoint Shaparak. He would be based there for the first part of his testing tour with 2 PARA – 2nd battalion, the Parachute Regiment. He lost one and a half stones trekking across rivers, ditches, ploughed fields and flooded cesspits, all while laden with up to 80 pounds of kit for himself and Memphis.

Shaparak was a rundown compound perched on the edge of a seething hotbed of insurgent activity. From this embattled location, he and Memphis conducted daily patrols. Their mission was to dominate the ground and limit the insurgents' freedom of movement.

As with all dog handlers, Mick had to put his buddy Memphis first and foremost. His routine after a gruelling patrol was to feed and water Memphis, clean his rifle, sort his own kit and wash. Then, and only then, he could think about getting a hot meal. Threat of attack was never far away. The compound's bunkers, known as sangars, boasted a wide array of weapons including General Purpose Machine Guns, Light Machine Guns and even Javelin anti-tank missiles.

Occasionally, Mick and Memphis would bound on to a helicopter to swoop down on an unsuspecting Taliban stronghold. The team would be dropped at the target compound at first light. Memphis would search up to the compound after an infantry cordon, a line of heavily armed soldiers, secured the immediate area. After the soldiers forced their way in, Memphis and Mick scoured the rooms. Sometimes, choppers would return to pick up the troops but occasionally Memphis and his comrades would wait for nightfall before trekking back to base. Mick said: 'It's not an easy task crossing fields and ditches using night vision. Harder still with Memphis dragging me around. On patrol, we split everything up. We'd be carrying batteries, extra water, first aid kit for the dog, food for the dog. You are carrying a fair bit of your own kit as well. You may be carrying extra ammo for the infantry guys.'

Every dog handler becomes an expert in multi-tasking, expected to look after themselves, their dog, and participate in the duties of an average rifleman. He said: 'The buck stops with you. You are the expert with the dog so you will have the dog's kit, food and anything else he needs. The dog's welfare is the top priority. They give us everything. We have boots, goggles, earmuffs, jackets that keep them cool. You soak the jacket with water and it takes the body heat away, keeps the dog cool. The kit we get is fantastic. Anything we want we can get. It's all about dog welfare. If there is a human casualty, they put out what they call a nine liner to get the soldier medevaced or medically evacuated. We have the same process for injured dogs, we have a canine nine liner. The vets are alerted so they will be there waiting for them when the helicopter comes in. At the end of the day, they are serving their country and they are part of the team.'

It was in the second half of this tour that the pair made their fateful trip to Toki. They were attached to Lima Company, 42 Commando, initially based at Checkpoint Lightning before moving south. This wildly peripatetic lifestyle tests the dog teams to the limit. A handler and his dog may be moved dozens of times throughout the tour, giving them less chance to bond with fellow soldiers but making a dog and handler even closer and more inseparable.

Mick said: 'Moving about all the time does bring you and the dog closer. Being a dog handler in the military is more of a vocation than a job because, on your days off, you still go into kennels and exercise the dog. It is very rarely that a day goes past that you won't see your dog. You have to be right into it.'

Mick also told me that military chiefs streamlined their procedures for deploying working dogs, so great was the demand for canines on the ground. RAF dog handlers were embedded with their Royal Army Veterinary Corps (RAVC) counterparts going on the same tour. This was a radical change to the past system where dog soldiers would arrive halfway through a tour, knowing no-one and being in the dark as to how their new unit operated.

It was clear to me that Mick is tortured by the fact that he will never deploy again, never again face adversity on the frontline with his comrades-in-arms. He faced a long, tortuous road to recovery. As he talked though, he began to sound more resolute. He confided to me that he had a new goal. To get Memphis back.

EIGHT

Canine chemistry

Science teaches us how Memphis, Benji and their four legged comrades are consistently such winners on the modern battlefield. Canine physiology and psychology, to be exact. As I immersed myself in the enormous literature of doggy science, I was in danger of being swamped by the sheer volume of research. For a while, my bedtime reading consisted of scintillating tracts such as: *A tale of two dogs: analysing two models of canine ventricular electro physiology* and *Comparison of Human and Canine Gastrointestinal Physiology*. Riveting reading, but the successful formula of soldier dogs can be reduced to two things, their remarkably sensitive noses and their unique bond with human beings.

In my bid to unveil what makes dogs tick and makes them so effective, I stumbled across the work of a band of dedicated researchers. These remarkable scientists are at the forefront of exploring the link between man and dog. Scientists at the Canine Cognition Centre at Duke University in North Carolina are unlocking the secrets of dogs' minds, uncovering ways to make them even more effective in 21st century conflicts. Fresh faced post-doctoral researcher Evan MacLean and his colleagues have made some remarkable discoveries including the fact that dogs are as smart as young children in their ability to understand non-verbal communication.

They are also working on a number of projects with the military, which Evan explains had to remain secret for operational reasons. On the Duke University website, he can be seen hugging a sleepy looking terrier to his chest. The dog loving scientist's research probes 'social cognition in dogs with a focus on how and what dogs understand about humans as social partners.' His studies aim to get 'a better understanding of the psychological mechanisms underlying dogs' social behaviour and apply findings to real world problems concerning dog-human interactions'. The latter part of that telling sentence reveals his key role in developing the next generation of military super-dogs and exploring the rich relationship between human and dog.

Speaking to me from his research lab, Evan explained that his work reveals what makes a dog's mind tick: 'We are looking at the way dogs deal with different problems so we can tailor an animal to a specific job. There could be an application for that in the military. We are dealing with the cognitive problems the dogs may have when they are at war. How does the dog's nose work? How do they navigate in strange and often dangerous environments? The dogs are using a lot of subtle psychological communication and interaction in their day to day lives and navigating in complex landscapes. Military working dogs are so useful because they have a combination of skills. The dog is a real package deal. If it was purely about their nose and their great sense of smell, then bloodhounds or even rodents would be deployed as they have a fantastic sense of smell.'

The other key part of the superiority of dogs is their ability to understand human communication. He added: 'If you compare dogs to other animals, they don't have all that great memories. They use their perceptual skills in communication roles. The dog has a bond with you and looks back to you for information. You can then use a dog as a tool. That is rare in the animal world.'

Canine chemistry

In years gone by, dogs were viewed as 'an artificial creation with unremarkable cognitive abilities' and were ignored from cognition studies in favour of primates. Now, however, they are a key focus in animal studies and have caught the imagination of linguists, evolutionary biologists, psychologists and anthropologists. Evan's cutting edge research has shown that dogs are more than mere learning machines, they have a rich understanding of their world which allows them to be flexible problem solvers. Incredibly, a dog's problem solving skills are so sophisticated that they resemble those of young children.

The Duke Canine Cognition Centre's research has taken Evan and his team from Africa to Siberia, where they compare dogs to a range of different species from domesticated apes and foxes to human-reared wolves. To properly understand the variations within dogs, they have worked with every type, from the smallest shelter puppy to the exotic New Guinea singing dog.

Evan's research is based around behavioural tasks, similar to the kind of work done by developmental psychologists. He said: 'We are looking at the dog's social skills and there is a lot of cross pollination between developmental psychologists and us. They work with pre-verbal kids in the same arena where we are working with animals.' Scientists have already managed to unravel the mystery of the genome of chimpanzees and revealed that humans are 96 percent similar in genetic terms. Evan and his comrades though, have proved that dogs are actually superior to many other species when it comes to reading human gestures and interacting with humans. Chimps are our closest living animal relatives but, according to Evan, dogs are much more like humans than people normally give them credit for.

His work confirms what dog owners the world over have known for years. Canines, much like humans, are individuals with their own foibles as well as distinct personal strengths and weaknesses. He told me: 'The human–dog relationship is a very close and personal connection. Dogs become attuned to their handler the same way they would with other dogs. Dogs are also individuals, there are differences not only between breeds but between each dog.

'Some are better than others at problem solving and can deal with problem A or B more effectively than another. Helping to identify these nuances could help tailor an animal to a specific job. A dog can also use its skills with any person, it doesn't necessarily have to be someone they know well. It will take directions and respond to someone making a following gesture by going to the right or left. Chimps do not communicate in the same co-operative way. Working dogs especially have an incredible bond with people and form a very close and personal relationship. They have special skills relative to other dogs such as seeing-eye dogs. Dogs use social information and have a real strength for navigation.'

It is the dog's sense of smell that really puts them a nose ahead of the rest of the animal kingdom. They have such an acute sense of smell that their exceptional noses are even being utilised to help detect cancers in humans. In 2011, German researchers discovered that sniffer dogs could be used to reliably detect lung cancer. Scientists published their findings in the European Respiratory Journal proving that trained dogs could detect a tumour in 71 percent of patients. Scientists are still baffled as to how dogs manage this remarkable feat. News that dogs could 'sniff out' cancer first came to light in 1989 and further studies have confirmed that dogs can detect some tumours such as skin, bladder, bowel and breast cancers. One theory is that tumours produce volatile chemicals which dogs can sense. Researchers trained four dogs, two German Shepherds, an Australian Shepherd and a Labrador, to detect lung cancer.

In the German experiments, three groups of patients were tested: one hundred and ten healthy people, sixty with lung cancer and fifty with chronic obstructive pulmonary disease, a narrowing of the airways of the lungs. They all breathed into a fleece filled tube, which absorbed any smells. Dogs then sniffed the tubes and sat down in front of the ones in which they detected the 'whiff' of lung cancer. They pulled it off 71 percent of the time. The study still begged the question: how did the dogs do it? Researchers lamented the fact that dogs may be good but unfortunately can't communicate to us the secrets of the biochemistry of cancer's scent.

Dogs are also now regularly being used to detect epilepsy and can even predict when their owner is about to have a seizure. My work as a journalist gave me the chance to hear about an extraordinary dog called Ebony. I was tipped off about the amazing story of the Collie cross who helped her owner overcome the nightmare of having up to 15 seizures a day. Corinna Murray told me that, thanks to Ebony, she hadn't suffered a seizure for months. The 34-year-old, who lives in Dumfries with her husband Willie, said: 'Ebony is amazing. I have no doubt she has played a large part in helping me to become seizure free recently. She can tell me in advance when I am about to have a seizure and this means that I can get myself somewhere safe before it happens. I was having up to 15 seizures a day and was suffering all sorts of injuries from falling over.'

Ebony is trained to warn Corinna and Willie 10 minutes before a seizure. She lies down and gives a special, urgent bark. Corinna said: 'Stress was often a trigger for my seizures and she certainly helps reduce that. The experts are not entirely sure how dogs like Ebony can pick up on a seizure before it happens. They think she could be spotting small physical changes.' The last time I spoke to Corinna she told me that Ebony was training to be a disability assistance dog that can help a patient when getting dressed, switching on lights, and even loading and unloading the washing machine.

World renowned canine expert Dr John Bradshaw, director of the Anthrozoology Institute at the University of Bristol, has studied the behaviour of domestic dogs for more than 25 years. He said: 'It's dogs' sense of smell that really distinguishes them from us. Their noses are so valuable to us. It's just the limits of human ingenuity and imagination that stop us from tapping into all their possibilities.'

Scientists have agreed that a dog's nose is a wonder of evolution. Olfaction, the act or process of smelling, is, without doubt, a dog's primary sense. Experts believe that a dog has hundreds of millions of olfactory receptors in its nose while humans have just a few million. A dog's nose consists of a pair of nostrils, known as nares, for inhaling smells, and a nasal cavity. Special odour detecting cells extend throughout its nasal cavity. Humans have slightly more than an inch and a half of a special tissue used to detect odours, known as olfactory epithelium, while some dogs have as much as 26 square inches of it.

The dogs' nasal mucous membrane has a rich supply of smell detecting nerves that connect with the brain's highly developed olfactory lobe. Dogs also boast an extra odour busting chamber called the vomeronasal organ that also contains olfactory epithelium. This distinctive piece of canine anatomy, known as Jacobson's organ, consists of a pair of elongated, fluid-filled sacs that open into either the mouth or the nose. It is found above the roof of the mouth and behind the upper incisors.

In a research paper entitled *The Dog's Sense of Smell*, animal scientist Julio E Correa explains the importance of this important part of a dog's make up. She says that olfactory cells in the vomeronasal organ also send impulses to a region of the dog's brain called the hypothalamus, which is associated with sexual and social behaviour. This organ is believed to be important in the detection of pheromones, body scents. This theory could account for the dog's ability to identify and recognize other animals and people so well.

'A dog's nose is normally cool and moist. The moisture secreted by mucous glands in the nasal cavity captures and dissolves molecules in the air and brings them into contact with the specialized olfactory epithelium inside the nose. Dogs use sniffing to maximize detection of odours. The sniff is actually a disruption of the normal breathing pattern. Sniffing is accomplished through a series of rapid, short inhalations and exhalations. Odour molecules in the olfactory epithelium of the nasal cavity are absorbed into the mucous layer and diffuse to receptor nerves. This interaction generates nerve impulses that are transmitted by the olfactory nerves to the dog's brain, which has a well-developed olfactory lobe. This allows the dog to recognize a scent and follow a trail.'

North America is a world leader in the use of working dogs. State and local law enforcement agencies have canine units trained to detect drugs and search for lost individuals, homicide victims, and forensic cadaver materials. US Customs and Border Protection has more than 800 canine teams that work with the US Department of Homeland Security to combat terrorist threats, stop the flow of illegal narcotics, detect unreported currency, concealed humans, or smuggled agriculture products.

American Beagle Brigade teams are also trained to passively indicate prohibited fruits, plants, and meats in baggage and vehicles of international travellers as they enter Federal Inspection Service areas in airports and ports. Britain is slowly catching up with the US, however, by grasping the utility, some might say necessity, of working dogs. Fire chiefs in the UK are now bringing in dog detectives to lend a paw to the fire service. The Association of Fire Investigation Dog Handlers provides several reasons why accelerant detection dogs are first class when investigating arson. According to the association, dogs detect the presence of ignitable liquids with greater sensitivity and accuracy than electronic field equipment, so increasing the detection of accelerated fire scenes. Canines can also differentiate between natural hydrocarbons produced during fires and hydrocarbons used in illegal fire setting. Canines can also cut the time an investigator spends on excavation and debris sampling.

Billy, who wears distinctive red protective shoes, is the latest addition to the growing army of fire service dogs around the UK. The Springer Spaniel is trained to sniff out petrol, acetone, diesel, lighter fluid, barbecue fluid and gel, white and methylated spirits. The lively pooch and his owner, former fire-fighter Duncan Carmichael, from Middlebie in Dumfriesshire, are card carrying members of the International Association of Arson Investigators. They have been invited to appear before top politicians at the Scottish Parliament to raise awareness of firefighting dogs. Billy can detect accelerant on wood up to seven days old. He was originally trained to be an explosives dog but was found to be surplus to requirements. Hundreds more dogs such as Billy could soon be battling blazes around the country, but it is in military duties that the benefit of working dogs easiest to see.

Dr Bradshaw says that dogs represent incredible valuable to the armed forces: 'I must say, if I was in an environment like that, I would actually much rather have a dog ahead of me than another human being because it's a different set of senses, and particularly the olfactory sense. These dogs are trained to find and then indicate all manners of things. In that particular instance, it would presumably be explosives and ammunitions and guns.' Dr Bradshaw, author of *Dog Sense: How the New Science of Dog Behaviour Can Make You a Better Friend to Your Pet*, said the bond between dog and handler was a joy to behold because they genuinely get on. He added: 'We have done some studies on how to get the best dogs. Since 9/11 in particular, the demand for sniffer dogs of all kinds has gone up many fold. So there has been a real supply problem.'

Dr Bradshaw has spearheaded new monitoring programmes to look at the best way to raise these dogs. 'They are very, very expensive dogs once they come to be fully trained. They are therefore very well protected in a combat zone. If you are going to put that amount of investment into an animal you need to be as absolutely sure as you can be that it's going to pay off, that you are going to generate a dog that is going to protect its handler and all the people around it. So we had a long look at puppies from the age of eight weeks up to a year or more to see what is the earliest point that the dog is suitable for training. We monitored how soon we could detect whether they were going to become a good training dog or not.'

Dr Bradshaw's work has even helped to dispel a few of his own misconceptions: 'I had imagined, as I think probably many people would, that the military used the same methods to train dogs as they did to train soldiers, which is to put them through hell. But they don't. Most of the military dogs – in fact, every dog I have ever seen or similar dogs in public service looking for narcotics in prison – is trained with positive reward. That woke me up to the fact that if the military, the hardest, toughest most macho guys around, can train dogs exclusively to do these tasks with reward based systems then surely everybody else can.'

It is the unique combination of a dog's ultra-sensitive nose and its unparalleled relationship with its human companions that have combined to make soldiers and canines such a winning team.

With 2700 dogs serving worldwide, the US military is at the forefront of research into serving dogs. Military Working Dog Adoptions founder Debbie Kandoll, who helps civilians adopt military working dogs, estimates that the average dog saves

150 soldier lives during its service. She said: 'These dogs are more soldiers than they are equipment. Equipment you can leave behind. We've left tanks in Iraq. Everywhere we've been, we've left stuff. If you reclassify them as manpower, then you can't leave them.' It has been estimated that the US Army left around 4900 dogs in Vietnam. Veterans believe that around 1600 were euthanized.

In 2000, President Bill Clinton signed a law that allowed the dogs to be adopted by former handlers, law enforcement agencies and civilians, but Ms Kandoll says the law must be updated to reclassify the country's dogs of war. US Representative Walter Jones of North Carolina is working on a bill that would reclassify the dogs as 'K-9 members of the armed forces' and provide a way for Pentagon chiefs to award the dogs with official medals. He summed up the feelings of soldiers around the world: 'Those who have been to war tell me that the dogs are invaluable. That they are just as much a part of a unit as a soldier or Marine. They are buddies.'

Under the current rules, if an American dog is retired on an overseas base, and is then adopted by a family in the United States, the adopter is charged the dog's shipping cost which can be as much as £4000. Ms Kandoll said: 'We have half-empty military cargo transport planes traversing the globe daily. It would be more than feasible to place a retired military working dog on the transport plane back to the continental United States. Uncle Sam got them over there and it's a point of honour for Uncle Sam to get his soldiers, whether they are four-legged or two-legged, back to the US.'

Some Brits have already taken steps to make sure our nation's own four legged veterans can live out their remaining years in comfort. I met an extraordinary soldier who not only brought one of his working dogs home but owed his life to a canine comrade.

NINE

In No Man's Land

Trapped in a confusing maze of compounds and alleyways with no sign of his mates, John Tucker checks his rifle and ammo while a wave of panic sweeps over him. Where the hell are they? The cold realisation sinks in, he is in the Taliban epicentre with no back-up. Their fighters pop up from this rat run of lanes to attack British troops before melting into the confusing network of back streets as quickly as they have come. In this corner of southern Afghanistan he is supposed to be escorted by a team of Royal Marines at all times, but they have vanished.

The old military cliché that no plan survives contact with the enemy is proving horrifyingly true. John has been in some hairy situations with his unit, 2 Royal Irish, but this is the most terrifying day in his career. Thankfully, he has an ace up his sleeve in the form of Rhett, a remarkable black Lab cross. John and Rhett have been tasked with searching a maze of alleys to find any weapons caches or IED making equipment.

It is February 2007, and they are spearheading an operation in the notorious town of Kajaki. Operation Kryptonite is the military name given to this mission to clear hordes of insurgents from around the Kajaki dam, a key facility which provides much of the power for Helmand province. NATO bombing attacks pound the Taliban day and night but still they will not give up. This mission is critical to the British and US effort in Afghanistan.

Commanders believe that holding the dam, ensuring the Afghan people have access to, at least, a limited amount of electricity will help win support for the Allied cause. British commander Colonel Tom Collins says that the Taliban do not intend to topple the dam but resort to a scorched earth policy, destroying everything in their tracks. He said: 'They destroyed or dismantled many of the complex mechanical components of the dam as they fled the field, to delay a NATO advance.'

Seizing this dam and getting it up and running again is of great importance to the Allies, as restoring much needed power to the area would win local support for the troops and the Afghan mission overall, as well as provide jobs in the energy sector.

As the Taliban consolidate their position in Kajaki, John and Rhett go into the lanes and compounds to flush them out. The pair are attached to 3 Commando Brigade which has just taken over the area from the soldiers of the Parachute Regiment. He told me: 'We had just deployed to Kajaki. The marines had attacked a village and we went in to clear. At first, the engineers were reluctant to use dogs because of the amount of munitions lying about. But the dogs are not stupid, they know it's there so I set them straight that it wasn't a problem.'

Marines spread out and take up firing positions to cordon off the area so that Rhett and John can move in. It should be a routine op for such an experienced duo but things quickly go wrong. With Rhett in front sniffing out any potential dangers, John focusses on staying calm as he edges down the lanes. A Taliban fighter, AK47 in hand, could jump out from any doorway or corner. Minutes seem like hours and John is slowly boiling under the weight of his body armour.

'We went quite far down the rat runs and then, at one point, I turned round and my escort was nowhere to be seen. You are always trying to watch the dog and read him so the escort of soldiers is there to back you up and keep an eye on you. To my horror, I realised I had lost them and the Taliban were preparing a counter attack.'

Lesser men might panic in a similar situation, running back the way they had come into a possible Taliban volley of fire or just breaking down and giving up. John however, tired and with the bitter tang of fear, surprise and adrenalin rising in his throat, looks down at Rhett and knows they will be alright. Rhett, with his warm brown eyes and white tuft of fur in the middle of his front paws, looks unfazed by the deepening crisis. He doesn't register the danger.

As the minutes tick by, John, despairing, even considers shooting his beloved dog to stop him from falling into the hands of the ferocious Taliban. If he was caught, he would suffer unspeakable torture before being killed and dumped into a rubbish pit.

Hearing shooting John questions what he is doing here. Can he retrace his steps or will he have to fight his way out? In the end, he decides that Rhett can lead them out. Letting him find a trail, he gives the dog the encouragement he needs to charge out of these deadly streets.

The pair move at a steady pace, breaking into a panicked run could lead them straight into the clutches of the Taliban. After what seems like hours, Rhett turns a corner leading them into the safety of an Afghan National Army cordon and John almost collapses with relief. He told me: 'The soldiers were just chilling out and smoking away so they got a bit of a surprise when we bolted round the corner. I was in the Army for 17 years and that was the one and only time that I did really, really worry. Thank God I had Rhett there.'

John has two dogs on his tour in 2006 to 2007, working with a Spaniel called Shai as well as Rhett. Both Rhett and Shai, who specialises in vehicle searches, will eventually be sent back to base in Germany and redeployed. 'They were absolutely great dogs,' he said. 'They had their own personalities, loved the jobs, and were a pleasure to work with. They both really loved the attention of the soldiers. Shai didn't mind helicopters and loved all the fuss. But no matter what I did Rhett always hated the Chinooks. When I was bringing him home, I had to carry him onto the flight.'

Although John and his charges will ultimately go their separate ways, he does get the chance to keep one of his other four legged comrades. Vehicle search dog Benji joined the father-of-two and his family at home in Lisburn, Northern Ireland, after a career defeating bomb making insurgents in Iraq. 'We rehomed in 2004 when he was about ten and a half years old. To get him back was fantastic, he was a liver and white Spaniel, brilliant with kids, very obedient, all that a typical Spaniel should be. He was 100 miles an hour, racing around everywhere.'

Benji gained an impressive reputation in Iraq for being a dog that never missed a trick. On one occasion, he found explosives ingeniously hidden in the wheel of a van at Basra airport. Benji sat bolt upright at one of the lorry's wheels and would not bat an eyelid, staring intently at the wheel rim. Bomb disposal experts moved the lorry to a safe area, where it was found to be laced with high explosives. His experiences in the killing fields of Iraq, though, left an indelible mark on Benji's psyche. Guy Fawkes Night in the UK became a living nightmare, a terrible reminder of his days on the frontline.

John says: 'I had Benji at home for three years. He used to get very scared with fireworks and I think that is because we used to get mortared a lot in Iraq. That affected him in some way. He would also become a shaking wreck with thunder and lightning and would run under our bed.'

Sadly, due to failing health, Benji had to be put to sleep at the grand old age of 13-and-a-half but, even as the years crept up on him, Benji never looked old and would bounce around like a younger dog. John's downcast face and sombre, halting tone is a testament to how close dog teams get. They are more than just a man working with yet another piece of military equipment.

'When Benji died,' John said, 'we were all absolutely heart-broken, I said I would never have another dog. I did not want to go through something like that again. My kids took it very badly. We still often talk about him. He was a true comrade.'

TEN

Dog Surge

I was deeply moved by John's emotional words about his dear Benji and by all the other tales of heroism I had uncovered about dogs and their handlers. So, I was eager to speak to the coalition commander who single-handedly launched the doggy surge, flooding Afghanistan with dogs like Memphis, Rhett and Benji to save human lives and limbs. Major Kevin Hanrahan is not very well known on this side of the Atlantic but he singlehandedly boosted numbers of military working dogs in Afghanistan, saving countless lives in the process.

Kevin calls himself an unashamed 'dog advocate', and is keen to make sure his troops have the tools they need to win the war, namely military dogs of all shapes and sizes. He has called his strategy 'paws on the ground'. I stumbled across his ultra-professional looking website as I boned up on the latest news of the NATO coalition's canine campaign in Afghanistan.

As Deputy Provost Marshal for US forces in Afghanistan he was responsible for around 1000 dogs, the biggest canine push in history. His strategy mirrored the much publicised military surge ordered by President Obama. In 2009, after the war in Afghanistan had dragged on for eight years, Obama and his advisers dreamed up the surge concept, flooding key areas in the south with soldiers to stifle the Taliban and bring stability.

President Obama came up with the scheme after he wandered

among the pristine white gravestones of Arlington National Cemetery in Virginia where the US buries its war dead, from the American Civil War to Afghanistan. Haunted by the enormous toll of young lives ruined by the war, he wanted to hasten the end of the conflict. He was reportedly humbled by hospital visits to wounded soldiers, telling aides: 'I don't want to be going to Walter Reed Hospital for another eight years.'

The crippling cost of the campaign was another factor. He received a memo estimating that the war could cost a mind-bending $1 trillion over 10 years. Under the surge, an influx of 30,000 United States reinforcement soldiers were deployed in southern Afghanistan and around Kabul. Major Kevin Hanrahan was responsible for the equivalent dog offensive.

After a brief exchange of emails, I managed to speak to him on the phone. Over the slightly echoey transatlantic connection, his Virginian drawl made him sound like a Civil War general. I had visions of him puffing on a cheroot as he took the call.

'Dogs are no longer simply pets,' he told me. 'They are family members. Military working dogs are no longer equipment. They are fellow warriors. Dogs are currently on the front lines in the fight against tyranny. They are saving soldiers' lives every day. As Deputy Provost Marshal for US forces in Afghanistan, one of my responsibilities was to oversee the military working dogs programme, a surge that is saving countless lives. Dogs are the number one combat multiplier on the ground today.

Kevin's passion for dogs as a military asset is infectious. He warmed to his subject as we chatted and I could picture him becoming increasingly animated as he espoused the value of his canine brainchild. He said: 'There is not a doubt they are making a significant impact on the battlefield. You really can't quantify one successful explosive find by a dog. Is it saving an arm, a leg, a life, is it saving half the squad? You just do not know but they are making an incredible impact. The enemy can't find anything to beat them. You *can't* beat instincts and a powerful nose.'

As the Taliban comes up with ever sneakier ways to cause carnage US and British dog teams up their game to combat the threat: 'We call it imprinting, the dogs are imprinted with home homemade explosives, so they are imprinted with ammonium nitrate, ammonium sulphite, whatever they are using downrange right now, we are imprinting our dogs with that. Metal detectors ain't finding it, but our dogs are. It's a great thing for us. There was a big push when I was trying to get more down to the south because that was where the main effort was last year.'

When Coalition forces pulled out of many southern provinces they left a power vacuum that the Taliban were all too eager to fill. The US moved several brigade combat teams into these areas but they lacked one vital component, dogs. The 37-year-old's description of the situation on the ground and the efforts of his dogs is punctuated by *My Gaaad!!!* and the occasional giggle as he reflects on how good the canine teams are.

He says dogs and their human comrades loved their work, despite the very real threat of death or serious injury: 'They come in and all they want is a pat on the head and a play with their ball, they are saving people's lives for a ball. It's so cool. What people don't quite understand is that you have a dog and a handler maybe 100ft ahead of the entire patrol. It's amazing to me.

'I've been a United States soldier since I was 18-years-old. The military isn't just my job, it's the way I live. I'm a Major in the US Army and have done three tours of duty in Iraq and Afghanistan. Everyone copes with the horrors and stresses of war differently. I write. I blog. I tell real stories and I channel what I've seen into novels.'

Kevin plans to pen a novel as a tribute to the men and

women in Afghanistan who are fighting and dying with the dogs that protect them. He became a firm dog advocate after his own dog 'saved my soul'. He has two Hungarian Viszlas, a sporting breed. When he got back from a tour of duty in 2005, he found his life in turmoil.

'My marriage was in a shambles. I had gone from being a company commander of 200 soldiers, they are your family. I was stationed in Germany and I had to give up company command, so I left my one family and get to states and my wife essentially leaves me. The only thing I have is my dog. I go from losing two families, leave a war zone with nothing and I have my dog. I feel like he saved my soul. I had so much love for dogs before reading Jack London books. I loved all the dog books when I was younger and dreamed of having dogs. That experience really cemented my love of dogs. The dog was called Sammy and it was just me and him for a long time.'

As commander of a major strategic push in Afghanistan, Kevin was annoyed that dogs did not get more credit. In November 2010, he was horrified to lose three dogs and three handlers in a week. He took the news hard: 'I thought, you have got to be kidding me? I mean these kids are on the frontline, they are doing heroic things, and people don't even know our dogs and dog teams are doing this. Someone needs to tell 'em. So I thought, I am going to write a book and I'm going to do it – just gonna do it. I had to spend about three days researching how to write a book because, I am a soldier, I don't know how to write a book.'

In his free time, he scoured the Internet for websites on writing and researching and, after a few days, started. He wanted to call his novel *Paws on the Ground*, in honour of the big offensive which he masterminded.

'I decided to write a fictional book because of the ethical challenges of non-fiction. I felt it would give me greater scope. I am a soldier first and foremost and can't give away specifics for operational reasons. Soldiering pays the bills and is my life, but I also feel very passionately that the public should know what dogs and dog handlers are doing in Afghanistan today.'

Kevin, who was awarded two Bronze Stars and an Army Commendation Medal for Valor, explained that the war in Afghanistan is far tougher than the campaign in Iraq. He said Iraq was civilised compared to Afghanistan. It is a real country. There was a structure before we got there; in Afghanistan there is just no structure. It's crazy. The literacy rates and the cultural difference are insane as well. The education of the Iraqi people is so much better than in Afghanistan. He told me: 'It's a mess over there. I really would love to think the work we put into it may have saved some lives. When you work in four star headquarters, it can be hard to look back and be like "hey, I made a great impact" but the dogs get quantifiable results on the ground.'

I could tell he was proud that his men, women and dogs have made a difference. Kevin now lives in rural Virginia with his wife Mehan and son Brady, plus his beloved dogs Sammy and Stella. His experiences have shown him how important it is to get dogs down to the soldiers fighting on the front-line. For him, soldiers must get access to the canines they need to win the war. He is also acutely aware of the sacrifice made by fellow NATO soldiers deployed in Afghanistan.

He told me how his stomach lurched as he read online about the death of British dog handler Liam Tasker. 'I thought, my God, who is going to tell the story of these dogs and their brave handlers?'

My next stop was the place where Liam and his dog Theo trained before they both died in Afghanistan.

ELEVEN

All roads lead to Melton

We hear it before we see it. My stoic partner Lynda and I have finally reached the Mecca of military working dogs, the Defence Animal Centre. The barrage of barking, high pitched and piercing even through the gusts of rain, is a dead giveaway. Mick, Memphis and hundreds of other dogs and their handlers have graduated from these hallowed kennels.

Tragic Liam Tasker and his beloved dog Theo also learned how to take on the Taliban here. Every British military dog team comes here to learn its trade, polishing lifesaving skills that will be tested to the limit when they hit the ground in Helmand. We are here at Melton to see history being made. For the first time in more than a decade, the centre is throwing open its kennel doors to the public. Army chiefs launched the open day to mark the Queen's Diamond Jubilee. So, on a squally, overcast Saturday at the start of June, we braved the 660 mile round trip from our home in the west of Scotland to Melton Mowbray in deepest, darkest Leicestershire.

The ever trusty satnav tells me that this expedition has taken the best part of six hours but, now, we have finally arrived. We set off at dawn, finally taking a circuitous route through fields with warning signs telling unsuspecting drivers to be wary of old mine works which were worryingly prone to collapse under a vehicle's weight.

After negotiating the pitfalls of England's rural food capital, it proved remarkably easy to find the Defence Animal Centre as hundreds of people of all ages were already congregating in the town. Military working dogs have clearly amassed quite a fan club. Melton Mowbray, famous for pork pies and cheese, could now add dogs to its growing list of attractions. It isn't yet 10.00 am and dogs are proving to be a major crowd-puller.

The day has a real festival feel with pipe puffing Royal Army Veterinary Corps veterans, complete with greying handlebar moustaches, rubbing shoulders with mums and dad carrying Hello Kitty clad toddlers on their shoulders. The Centre, or DAC, given the Army's enduring love of acronyms, sprawls over miles of flat countryside at the back of an anonymous housing estate. A young woman soldier with curly blonde hair peeking out from under her beret, greets us as we enter the base. This twenty-something handler, whose name is Sue, is not long back from a tour of duty in Afghanistan.

How did you find the heat and the danger? I ask, as we head towards a one story kennel block that seems suspiciously quiet.

'It was great to get out there and do the job that I had trained so long to do,' she tells me. 'It's a brutal environment for all the guys but you definitely feel safer when you have one of the dogs with you. It's really draining to have to watch every step you take, not only looking out for yourself but for your dog too, to make sure it isn't knackered, or flagging because it's thirsty.' She said that being kept apart from friends and family for six months in the middle of a dangerous desert was a nightmare. 'Everyone misses their family and friends when they go to Afghan but I wouldn't change my job for anything. To be in the Army and work with dogs is a dream.'

Blue eyed Sue looks young for her age. Despite being clad in the mottled brown, green and beige Army uniform, she wouldn't look out of place at a Justin Bieber concert. Her youthful enthusiasm shines through as we tour a brand new kennel complex. Its bars are still gleaming and the floors are spotless, unsullied by muddy paws. In her soft Midlands accent, she tells us: 'These are the new kennels that have just been built, we are going to keep the sick dogs here next to the vets. None have moved in yet, that's why the place is so immaculate. I was amazed at the care they get. There was a dog called Fire who was really badly injured in an IED blast in Afghanistan. He came back here to Melton and after loads of veterinary care, and a healthy dose of TLC, made a full recovery.'

Staff are poised at this doggy intensive care section 24 hours a day, every day of the year, to make sure dogs like Fire get back on their paws. Vets and veterinary technicians are on call to deal with any emergency; it is, in effect, a canine casualty ward. The kennels have heating for winter and air conditioning for clammy summer days. What's the best and worst part of the job?

'It's hard seeing the dogs when they are injured, your heart goes out to them,' she says. 'The best is seeing the love between the handlers and their dogs. They are working dogs and a military asset, but there is a massive bond. Seeing the dogs work and the care they get, made me want to do this. They really are loved; no doubt about it.'

We see just how well loved these military working animals are as we walk around the site of the veterinary training squadron. A touching memorial to war horse Sefton is tucked away just off the entrance road to the Army School of Equitation, overlooking a panorama of verdant fields. He was a striking, black horse who was part of an unsuspecting Blues and Royals Mounted Squadron that rode out from Hyde Park barracks in July 1982 into the killing zone of an IRA bomb. As Sefton trotted towards Hyde Park Corner an IRA nail bomb was detonated, killing four soldiers and seven horses and leaving others with horrific physical and psychological injuries.

Sefton was 19-years-old, the oldest of the horses. His injuries were gruesome: his jugular vein was severed and a six-inch nail went through his bridle. Vets feared that he may not survive but after 28 pieces of shrapnel were removed from his body, he made a gradual but complete recovery and was well enough to go back on parade the following November.

Horse lover Jilly Cooper, better known for her romantic novels, was a big fan. She paid tribute to him at the time of his death: 'He became a national symbol of courage and stoicism. I went down to see him at Melton Mowbray when he was recovering. All the other horses were jumpy and nervy, biting and kicking people, but Sefton was completely calm and phlegmatic. I gave him lots of barley sugar and he was getting sack-loads of fan mail. He was absolutely gorgeous. When he died, years later at 30, the trooper who was looking after him was in floods of tears, like so many of us, and uttered the immortal line, 'St Peter won't need to open the pearly gates, because old Sefton will fly over them'.

After retiring from the Household Cavalry in 1984, he was moved to the Home of Rest For Horses at Speen, Buckinghamshire. When he died, his body was moved here to his final resting place at the Defence Animal Centre. A small sign at the side of his grave tells his story: 'Sefton endured eight hours of surgery, a record length for horse surgery in 1982. Each of his 34 wounds was potentially life-threatening; some included dislodging shrapnel from bone.'

The evening after surgery the veterinarians gave him a fifty-fifty chance of surviving the shock and extreme blood loss. Over the next months he made continual progress and his nurse was quoted thus, 'He took everything in his stride.'

During his time in hospital he received huge quantities of cards and mints, his favourite treat. Members of the public donated almost £500,000 to construct a new surgical wing at Royal Veterinary College which was named the Sefton

Surgical Wing. Two pictures of Sefton flank his gravestone. One black and white snap shows him in playful mode, nuzzling the face of one of the troopers while the other colour picture, on the right hand side, shows him sporting a large red, white and blue rosette next to a soldier in ceremonial dress. A small posy of fresh pink, crimson and white flowers sits next to his stone. The inscription reads: 'Sefton – A brave cavalry horse who survived the bombing outrage in Hyde Park on 20th July 1982.' The polished grey stone sits at the head of a large oblong covered with small stones. There is not a weed in sight.

Further down the road we enter the veterinary training squadron, the hub of the whole centre. Our open day programme describes it thus: The smallest of the training elements at the DAC but at the heart of all activity, it is this department that ensures that best veterinary practise is maintained and animal welfare is never compromised. The centre boasts another three squadrons: headquarters, and the canine and equine training squadrons. Each year 700 students from across the British military and 250 animals embark on more than thirty different courses. Dogs are checked here to make sure they have no underlying health problems that will hamper their Army careers.

Walking into the doggy hospital is like venturing into a smaller version of any human surgical facility. Gleaming surgical tools, blue green infection control aprons, clinical white X-ray machines and anaesthetising apparatus would look familiar to any patient. Only the muzzles hanging from a shelf and the strong meaty whiff of dog food give the game away. This is no ordinary diagnostic and surgical centre for two legged patients.

Lynda reels back in shock as she peers into the kennels of the intensive care unit. She approaches a tall, imperious looking corporal who is escorting members of the public around the facility. 'Er, excuse me, I think one of the dogs is really unwell,' Lynda says as she leads him to the kennel door opposite a long window allowing vets to keep an eye on their convalescing charges. After a quick glance, the corporal replies: 'Ma'am, everything is fine, that dog is actually a dummy.'

This raises a laugh with the other visitors. The corporal shows us around, pointing to a whiteboard with a litany of veterinary terms detailing the dog patients and their injuries. One name leaped out at me – *Crazy*. I stifle a laugh as I ask: 'Crazy by name, crazy by nature?' He grimaces: 'Yep, I am afraid so. He is as mad a box of frogs. He bounces about all over the place; that's actually why he was in here a while back. He was jumping around and managed to damage his tail. He was in here for a partial tail tip amputation. If the surgeons can, they will try and save as much of the tail as possible. Sometimes they may have to remove it all because of infection but that's rare.'

A light box on the wall is covered with X-rays of a dog's leg. Even to the untrained eye, it is apparent that the leg has been damaged, a large, ragged split runs down through the bone. There are before and after images. The X-rays show that the dog had been fitted with pins to hold the bone together until it can fuse of its own accord. Another minor miracle in this place. The dog is apparently now fighting fit.

Outside in the rain, a lance corporal with a shaven head and a distinctive brogue is drawing appreciative gasps as he puts an arms and explosive search dog called Pivo through his paces. He pushes his wire framed glasses up his nose as he explains what the dog can do. With the soft burr of a South African accent, he says: 'When we are training the dogs, we cut up a toy and get them to search for smaller and smaller parts of the toy. By the end, they can easily find a piece that is small as a grain of sand. We have to be careful because at the end, the piece is so small the dogs could hoover it up their noses.'

Dogs are weaned from searching for their toys to more deadly substances such as TNT, Cordtex, C-4 and Semtex. Once they pick up a scent and indicate to the handler where it originates, by sitting or lying and staring at the spot, their toy 'magically' appears out of thin air. In reality, the handler takes it from his pocket and throws it at the source of the scent. This process is fine in training but, clearly, in Afghanistan, handlers are not keen to throw toys or any other objects at 500 pound IEDs. The dog get his reward later, in a safer position.

Pivo, our demonstration dog today, is a wiry, black and brown Belgian Malinois with a jaunty gait. He struts around the Army issue green tent as we huddle to watch him in action. The ground in the tent has been covered with fine sand while large concrete breeze blocks have been stacked two or three high facing the entrance. Motes of dust swirl in the air as Pivo sits aloof, next to another handler, pointedly ignoring us and four other onlookers.

'Right, I will send Pivo outside so he can't see where I place the piece of this toy,' the South African says, holding up a tiny red speck with a pair of tweezers. The speck has been cut from a rubber dog toy. 'I won't even touch the piece with my hands in case Pivo picks up my scent. We have to watch all the time, the dogs are so clever they will pick up any changes, even small changes in our body language. They will pick on the body handler's stance or whatever and that will give them an indication. We don't want to do anything to prejudice them latching on to a scent.'

Once Pivo is outside the tent, a young boy gets to pick where wants the fragment to be placed. Once he chooses his spot, the lance corporal uses a metal hook to pick up the breeze block where the piece will be stashed. This is another move designed to stop his own scent giving the game away.

With his nose in the air, Pivo trots back into the tent. His handler bends over him and with an exaggerated sweep of his hand, tells him to search. This move lets the dog know that it's time to put his game face on. Play time is over, something clicks in Pivo's mind and he is off. His head is down and his muzzle begins twitching in and around the concrete blocks. He moves with purpose at a deliberate pace as his handler pal follows, clutching his lead. Pivo strains against a sturdy looking harness consisting of a collar with a strip of webbing linked to a strap around his chest. He noses around the blocks, always moving forward, sifting the air through his damp, black nose. As he approaches the hiding place, his demeanour changes. He looks even more focussed as he picks up the scent.

He has locked on to the smell a couple of metres away from the exact spot. Edging nearer, he moves faster with what appears to be greater concentration. Then, there is a Eureka moment. He sits on his hind legs, his head down, staring at a concrete block, the very one the little boy picked. Our South African pal says: 'We train the dogs to give a passive indication when they make a find. The dogs can be trained to indicate a find by barking or lying down or whatever. Obviously, barking wouldn't be too good in a combat situation as Mr Taliban could hear you miles away. Also, training the dog to lie down as an indication is not necessarily too good when there are loads of mines and IEDs around. For our purposes, this kind of passive indication, where Pivo sits and stares, is ideal.'

Just then, Pivo's handler gives his harness a yank, trying to pull him away. He tugs it once more and claps his hands, making noises to distract the dog. The result is the same no matter what he does. Pivo is resolute, unmoved. He stares intently at the spot where the toy fragment is hidden. A ripple of applause resounds around the tent as we marvel at Pivo's skills. The lance corporal tells his comrade to take the dog for a drink and a well-earned rest: 'He will get a lie down and have some water or a bite to eat. Keeping an eye on your dog is absolutely vital in Afghanistan. If the dog's tongue is hanging out and he looks tired and thirsty, his performance will deteriorate. It's just the same as a human. If you are working hard but you are not hydrated and well rested, your performance will drop off pretty quickly. If your dog is not at the top of his game, bad things can happen. He could make a mistake and someone could get hurt, so a good handler is always looking out for his or her dog at all times. It's important in theatre to monitor the dogs; they are far less effective when they are tired.'

South African Hans (not his real name) joined the Army as a foot soldier but was so impressed that he became a dog handler at the first opportunity: 'It was in the infantry that I saw the dogs operating in Afghanistan. It was totally life changing for me when I saw what they are capable of. I thought "that is for me". People just don't realise how good they are and how important they are on the ground. Everyone gets carried away with laser guided missiles and all these high tech gizmos but it's the dog teams who are saving people all day, every day and helping to beat the Taliban. It's terrible that the public are not better informed about what our dogs and handlers do. They really are forgotten heroes out there.'

He says the dogs lifts the morale of soldiers far from home: 'It gives the guys a boost and it's good to have a mutt that is so reliable, loveable and totally pleased to see you. At the end of the day, who doesn't love a dog?'

Most people in the UK, famed for being a nation of animal lovers, will agree.

War in Afghanistan, though, has thrown up a horrific new development. A chilling tactic has emerged, the cold blooded, deliberate targeting of Army dogs by Taliban fighters. Audiences around the world recoiled in horror as they viewed the carnage of 9/11 on their TV screens. The attacks on the Twin Towers in New York and on the Pentagon made it clear that international terrorists do not respect geographical, physical or moral boundaries. Now, it seems, they have reached another morally repulsive low by disregarding the sanctity of animal life.

Hans flinches as he recalls seeing the Taliban targeting working dogs: 'We were out on patrol and picking up *icom* chatter, which is Army speak for the Taliban yacking on their walkie-talkies. One of the Taliban commanders saw my dog and me moving and he was shouting: "Take them out, take them out, get the dog first!" It was scary, they knew where we were and were desperate to kill us. They just hate the dogs, they can't beat us in a stand up firefight so they use roadside bombs and booby traps but our dogs are the biggest IED killer we have. They hate the dogs, really hate them.'

I am already all too aware of the chilling toll this Taliban tactic has already taken on British forces. Fellow Scot Liam Tasker was killed after a sniper tried to assassinate his Spaniel, Theo, who had sniffed out a record breaking haul of bombs and weapons. The world of military working dogs is a small one so everyone I meet is devastated by Liam's death. When he was killed in March 2011, brave Theo also died from a seizure. Many commentators thought that the dog had died of a broken heart after seeing his beloved human pal killed in action.

Theo had launched a bomb sniffing blitz against the Taliban, unearthing a record 14 IEDs in the first five months of his Afghanistan tour. Theo trained here at the Defence Animal Centre. The first stage consisted of 16 weeks' basic training and assessment before he was given to a handler. Theo and Liam then spent 15 weeks on a specialist handlers' course where they learned to work as a team. Their remarkable record made them a target for the insurgency. When he died, Liam's pal said: 'Soldiers on the patrol believe that the insurgent was trying to kill Theo to prevent a stash of IEDs being found. Liam was an incredible soldier and it was his professionalism, bravery and dedication that made Theo such an amazing search dog.'

The 22-month-old Springer Spaniel cross came under a hail of gunfire during the attack that killed Liam in the Nahr-e Saraj area of Helmand.

Just weeks before his death Liam, of Kirkcaldy, Fife, said: 'I love my job and working with Theo. He has a great character and never tires. He can't wait to get out and do his job and will stop at nothing.'

Major Caroline Emmett paid tribute to Liam: 'He and his dog had more operational finds than any individual team has had in Afghanistan to date and he saved many lives as a result. He was so proud of his achievements and I was so proud of him. He died a hero, doing a job he loved.'

Liam was the 358th British soldier to die in Afghanistan since operations began in October 2001. At the time, his family said he had died a hero doing a job he was passionate about. The statement read: 'We are so proud of him and everything he's achieved. Words can't describe how sorely he will be missed.'

As we walk outside the demonstration tent at the Defence Animal Centre, Hans says that everyone here was broken hearted by the loss of Theo and Liam. 'We are quite a close knit family so it was a big blow. Just last month, they had a rugby match in his memory. He was a great guy and so well thought of by everyone. Theo was a terrific dog too, so good at his job. We all know the dangers we face but it's never easy to handle losing one of your own.' He pauses, takes off his glasses, rubs his eyes and squints into a glimmer of sunshine that pokes through the dour looking sky.

Taliban attacks on army dogs have soared with many incidents being reported by other coalition forces. While in Melton, I discover that a much loved Australian Army dog called Quake has been killed during a firefight. Four-year-old Quake was struck by a hail of bullets during an attack by Australian Special Forces on a bomb-making factory. His handler was hurt but survived. Quake's death left his human comrades devastated. His body was returned to a multinational base in Tarin Kowt, southern Afghanistan, before his ashes were sent home to Australia.

US forces, which make up the bulk of the NATO force in Afghanistan, have suffered numerous attacks on their soldier dogs. On April 9, 2012, an American soldier took a bullet in the leg as he tried to protect his dog, Bart, which had been deliberately targeted. US Army Sergeant Aaron Yoder received a gunshot wound as fighters tried to take Bart out during a firefight in troubled Maiwand district, Kandahar province, southern Afghanistan. Yoder dived over Bart to protect him once the battle erupted. They were patrolling for IEDs when a horde of Taliban tried to kill the black Labrador retriever. Bart was unhurt in the attack but his fellow soldiers had to drag Yoder to safety before he was medevaced by helicopter to an Army hospital.

In Iraq in 2004, insurgents put a price on the head of Melton Mowbray based Army dog Blaze. The English Springer Spaniel was the target of the assassination bid after finding bombs, AK47s and other deadly weapons used against British soldiers. The contract was put on Blaze's head by militiamen loyal to Saddam Hussein, and an insurgent tried to kill him as he worked next to a road in Az Zubayr, south-west Basra. The assassin deliberately swerved and tried to knock the dog over before speeding off. Blaze escaped with just cuts and bruises and lived to fight another day.

At the time, a senior Army officer said: 'There is no doubt that this was a deliberate assassination attempt. Bounties are commonly offered in Iraq and we are convinced that there was a price on Blaze's head.'

Handler Lance Corporal Steve Dineley remains convinced that the contract was put out after two-and-a-half year old Blaze discovered heaps of guns, bullets, grenades, bombs, dynamite and even five anti-aircraft guns. Thankfully, he made a full recovery back here at the centre.

At Melton, our day's highlight is meeting Bracken, a livewire Spaniel who clearly loves his job. He is like a sniffing, panting blur as he flashes past me, a veritable gold and tan furry dynamo. He may be small but he moves fast as he runs around, hard on the trail of a scent which my inadequate human nose can't even detect. Here is a veteran arms and explosives dog in action, and woe betide anyone who calls him a 'sniffer dog'. His handler makes it clear: 'These aren't sniffer dogs, all dogs sniff and these aren't just any old dogs.'

One thing is for sure, Bracken looks bewildered by all the attention he is getting. It is, after all, a Saturday. This is usually a much deserved day off for him and the others. It is normally spent lazing around with the odd hour or two playing with a favourite toy. As Bracken zigzags around the grass field, he looks a tad perplexed by such a throng on his day off. By rights, he should be having an afternoon nap but here he is instead, the star of the show.

His cute looks and cream, gold and tan colouring are real crowd pleasers. Cooing mums and young boys and girls are eager to give him a rub behind the ears. We elbow our way through the crowd to get a look at him as he races around the training area, covered in uncut grass and dotted with old tyres and broken paving stones. It is a trek to get up here to see Bracken do his stuff. The centre at Melton sprawls over miles of countryside. Hordes of families with prams and wheelchairs look like pilgrims as they set out to negotiate the scrabbly rock track between the Veterinary Training Squadron and the Canine Training Squadron.

This impromptu assault course does not put people off. By far the biggest draw of the day is here at the outlying dog training section. Scores of people squeeze together to get the inside

119

track on Bracken's skills. As an arms and explosives search dog, he has completed a number of operational tours of duty. Sweeping his hand over a wide variety of weapons including AK47 machine guns, rocket propelled grenades (RPGs) and what appears to be an old British Army self-loading rifle (SLR), Bracken's handler Ben (again not his real name), says these are just a few of the weapons that the dog can find. 'He is a pleasure to work with but is a bit shy of people he doesn't know and he might be a bit spooked by all the people around today.' Dogs like Bracken hunt weapons but also find explosive substances such as TNT, Cordtex, C-4 and Semtex.

Within seconds of his toy being hidden, he is on to it like a scent seeking missile. We are given a quick master class beforehand on the factors affecting a scent trail. A quick scan of my dog-eared notepad tells me there are eight variables which affect how a dog picks up a scent. Various factors come into play such as the quantity of explosives; the bigger the amount of target material the stronger the scent. Time is also an issue, the longer a bomb is hidden, the stronger and more vivid the scent picture becomes in the dog's mind. Heat has to be taken into account. Warm air causes the scent to rise and expand while cold weather causes it to fall and contract. Different substances have their own scent signatures which vary from very small, and difficult to detect, to very large and able to be sniffed out easily. The age of a substance also dictates the strength of the scent that it emits. It sounds blindingly obvious but wind, air currents and draughts will carry scent away from the source causing a dog to become confused.

Paradoxically, any bad guy who tries to mask the scent of his weapons cache could actually be helping the dog teams. A strong scent where it is not expected is a red flag to a dog like Bracken.

Finally, the location of bombs or any other target items will affect how much scent is allowed to come out to waft into the dog's nose. For example, a target will be harder to find if it is stored underwater rather than in a cupboard in a house. Bracken, of course, does not know any of this. He just wants his toy and he wants it right now. His incessant scurrying across the landscape may seem a bit random to the untrained eye, but he is working systematically to draw a three dimensional scent picture of his environment. He is 'seeing' the smell of his beloved toy.

Meanwhile, a strange looking, shiny device lying on the ground catches the eyes of the curious kids in the crowd. 'What's that big wheel?' a pink cheeked girl asks her mum. She, like the rest of us, is stumped for an answer. The metal contraption looks like an alloy car wheel that had been over-stretched. Its twelve spindly arms meet at a small container resembling a pepper pot without the holes in the lid.

This carousel is seven or eight feet in diameter but only stands a few inches off the ground. Unknown to us, this device is specially designed for training dogs to detect IEDs in Afghanistan. Each of the arms holds a pot that is used to hold the target item. Out of sight of the dog, a piece of cut up toy is placed in one of the pots. Once Bracken is brought back and told to 'search' with the sweeping hand movement, he is on to the scent in seconds. He targets the pot and sits staring at it. Cue a big reward, namely his toy and a play with his handler. As Bracken's handler throws his toy on to the source of the scent, so that the toy appears, magically, before Bracken's eyes, he explains the curious paradox at the heart of working with these military dogs. 'On one hand, these dogs are so intelligent and do things that humans can't, but on the other hand, they can be a bit daft, believing that their toy materialises out of thin air. I suppose that is one of the quirks that makes them so appealing. They can be sharp as a tack and daft as a brush at the same time.'

During my trek across the canine training area, I discover

quickly that the Kong is King in the military dog world. Kongs are hard rubber toys that look like three balls fused together in a snowman shape. They are ubiquitous, and are found literally everywhere that you find military working dogs. The Defence Animal Centre is no exception. They are hanging out of dog's mouths, perched on tables of dog equipment, hanging off signs showing what the dogs can do.

Dog expert Maria Goodavage reveals that the training and handling of military working dogs today just wouldn't be the same without the Kong. She says: 'A handler told me about the first bomb dog he had. The dog was a veteran and knew exactly what was expected of him. "He'd be like – Get my Kong ready and get set to praise me up and I'll go find a bomb for you." When you think of what this rubber toy inspires, it's just incredible.'

Retired working dog Fritz inspired the whole Kong phenomenon. The former police dog turned up his nose up at the usual chewable items such as shoes and purses and preferred gnawing on sticks, stones and other potentially dangerous objects. Kong inventor Joe Markham was at his wits end as Fritz's teeth were worn down by the daily dental assault. While working on his old Volkswagen bus, Joe began throwing out car parts to Fritz to lure him away from those rocks. A rubber suspension part took Fritz's eye and lured him away from the stones. The dog plopped it in Joe's lap, licking his hand and eager to play, and Joe was inspired by the rubber item's erratic bounce and toughness.

Dog training would never be the same again. Joe drew up a design and found a rubber manufacturing factory near his home in Colorado. His business partner saw the prototype toy, declaring that it looked like an earplug for King Kong. So, the name was born.

Kongs of all shapes and sizes seemed to be at every kennel and training facility I visited, with hundreds in use at the

Defence Animal Centre. Red is the most popular colour in military circles although a black version exists. From Faslane naval base in Scotland to Camp Bastion, Afghanistan, these toys are everywhere. The company donates boxes of the toys each year to dog facilities and handlers. In a bizarre twist, Kongs are now also being used with wolves, wild dogs and even Tasmanian Devils in an Australian zoo.

After my Melton trip, dog behaviour and training specialist Mark Hines, who works for the Kong Company at their HQ in Colorado, let slip how the toys are now being used with an incredible array of animals. He clearly loves his work and his enthusiasm for Kongs and their role in doggy training is obvious. He says: 'Military handlers, like us, see the toys as tools for behaviour modification. We do a lot of work with handlers in the UK, in fact we just donated a lot of Kongs to handlers who will be working at the Olympic Games in London. The company has always had a close affinity with the military and law enforcement because that's where it all started. Fritz was an ex-police dog and was bored to tears. Once he developed the Kong from an axel stop, Fritz couldn't get enough of it. No matter where Joe Markham would hide it, Fritz would find it.'

Mark knows exactly the Kong's secret, what makes them so exciting for dogs. 'Kongs have an erratic bounce that stimulates the dogs and keeps them focussed. They will find explosives or whatever to get that Kong. The Kong is also 80 percent natural rubber and, because of its cone shape, it really satisfies the dog's need to chew. We would say that they are satisfying a predatory need in a domestic way. These dogs really chomp down on the Kong like it's a pacifier. Dogs think "Give me my Kong, I will find what you want if you just give me my Kong". They will work their entire life for a toy.'

As Mark explains, Kongs dominate the dog toy market and only have one real competitor, the tennis ball. He says: 'Sure, tennis balls are cheaper but when they get wet they pick up sand and dirt which wears down a dog's teeth. German Shepherds, Labrador Retrievers, Belgian Malinois and Belgian Shepherds make up about 90 percent of military dogs because of their drive and energy. A dog like that knows he wants his toy and will do anything to get it. Some trainers used a small jack-in-the-box style machine with their Kongs to reinforce the link between the toy and the target scent of arms and explosives. They have this remote control device with a number of boxes. Once the dog sits at the odour you want it to find, you push a button and the Kong pops up, reinforcing the connection between the Kong and the scent in the dog's mind.'

It's a neat trick. You want the reward to appear to come from the odour.

British handlers that I spoke to threw the Kong on or near the target scent to achieve the same effect. In Afghanistan, the dog's gratification was delayed by operational necessity and by the need to avoid handlers throwing objects about in a potential IED or minefield. Handlers are often the weak link in the chain, according to Mark, passing on their weaknesses down the leash to the dog. 'We often have issues with the handler. It can be the handler who messes up the dog. They may have problems with "not outing" the Kong or they may not get the timing right and it affects the dog.'

Kongs come in three types: black, red, which seems to be most popular at the Defence Animal Centre, and blue which contains barium and will show up on X-rays if swallowed by accident. Military dogs are so well trained with Kongs that explosives and narcotics have been placed in a Kong warehouse with millions of toys and the dog still hones in only on the target scents of drugs or bombs. Dogs are fascinated with the Kong's erratic bounce and its 'mouth feel'. Kongs seem to stimulate their drive to play and seek out prey at the same time.

A British Army handler at the centre sums up the attraction: 'I don't know what it is about them but the dogs all seem to love Kongs. They don't bounce in the normal way around ball does, they bobble and skip all over the place. It seems to trigger something in the dog's mind, perhaps it resembles an injured bird or rabbit and the underlying hunting instinct kicks in. They also love the chewy feeling in their mouth. They can't get enough of it.'

Military dogs still get other toys, such as tennis balls, for rewards. Even a rolled up sock will do but, in military circles, as often as not, it will be a Kong. 'We are so proud to help people and dogs that are risking their lives out there on the frontline,' Mark says. 'It is immensely satisfying for everyone here to know that Kong is the toy of choice for handlers and dogs.'

Back at the centre, a deadly IED sits in full view waiting to kill and maim any unsuspecting passers-by. Fortunately, this one is a realistic looking mock up which has been sliced in two to show the chilling efficiency of the Taliban's bomb-makers. We stare in awe at the fiendish looking model. The mock up bomb is perched on a table, just a few hundred yards from a couple of mock suburban houses used to train the dogs in an urban environment. If this device was real, it could have killed everyone nearby and wrecked the surrounding homes. The display is a stark reminder why millions of pounds have been lavished on this centre. Dogs and their handlers are risking their lives tackling devices like this one, every day.

The simulated IED consists of a white detergent bottle with two white wires leading to a battery. Another tangle of wires leads to two wooden plates under a surface covering of sand and grit. The whole device is encased in a brown wooden box with a glass window at the front to allow people to get a look at the bomb's inner workings. This cross-section of a bomb gives us a glimpse of the kind of pressure plate device currently being used against UK and NATO forces in Afghanistan. It is buried with the pressure plate just under the surface.

A soldier explains that the pressure plate contains two metal components. When these parts are pressed together by the weight of a passing soldier or vehicle, the electrical circuit is completed and carnage results. This display bomb simulates a one kilogramme charge. Some of the IEDs in Afghanistan can be hundreds of times bigger. The power source is located under the explosive charge, a deliberate ploy by the bomb makers. They deliberately bury the power source as deeply as possible to foil the metal detectors used by search teams. Dogs, however, can still find these bombs.

Later, a Belgian Malinois appears to grin at the camera as he jumps into what looks like an overgrown paddling pool. Another shot shows a handler petting his dog as they sit in the shade of a truck to escape the blazing Afghan sun. We watch in silence as the images flick up on the screen while a pop music soundtrack, Elton John to be precise, blares through speakers at the side of the room. A handler is showing a home movie of snapshots from her Afghan tour on an overhead projector in one of the centre's lecture theatres.

There is a series of *awws* and *ahs* from the crowd of onlookers, mainly mums and dads with their anorak wearing youngsters. The silence is penetrated just once after an angelic, curly haired boy points to a large jar on a shelf at the side of the room, containing a spherical, gruesome looking medical specimen and asks, 'Mum, is that a testicle?'

Stifling a laugh, I walk around the small, rectangular por-takabin as the slideshow starts again to a new audience. A group of anatomical drawings on the wall display a dog's physiology. Some pictures on the wall from medical textbooks are stomach churning: a dog with a horrendous flea infestation which clogs his ears, a horse with painful gashes across his nose. I gaze out the window at the crowds that weave through the stables and kennels. More than 3000 people, laden with plastic ponchos and a rainbow of umbrellas, have come here for the open day.

Drizzle streams down the pane as the weather takes a turn for the worse. Lynda's ensemble of heels and turquoise dress seems to be a tad foolhardy. I watch as a stall emblazoned with 'I Am a Civilian, Get Me out of Here!' attracts a steady throng of young boys eager to don a blindfold and plunge their hands into covered boxes holding a variety of gross substances. I never actually get to find out what exactly is in the boxes but I heard a female corporal jokingly tell a horrified youngster that one contained doggy saliva. Despite the metallic grey sky threatening more rain, there is a real carnival atmosphere.

It is clear that the UK's defence chiefs now see the wisdom of spending cash on these dogs. From the portable 'sky-kennels' used to house them on the long journey to Afghanistan to the first class veterinary facilities, it is obvious that taxpayers' cash is being well spent. The Centre, however, has suffered its fair share of criticism over the years. In the past, it was the focus of a media storm with claims of misspent money and squalid conditions. In 2011, MoD officials were pilloried for allowing the cost of a massive refurbishment to soar out of control.

Newspaper reports said that kennels would cost more than five-star hotel rooms under a controversial Private Finance Initiative (PFI). Officials were criticised after an £11m contract for new dog accommodation, stables, training facilities, and staff housing at the centre had spiralled. Over 25 years, taxpayers signed up to pay £109 million for the deal. One newspaper probe claimed that with about 50 dogs and 10 horses in training at any one time, this worked out at about £200 per night per kennel just for accommodation, while double rooms were available at the five-star London Hilton for £40 less.

PFI contractor Realm was awarded the contract in 2000 but six years later the kennels still weren't ready. In 2008, the Centre was again rocked after losing its licence to keep dogs when the facilities were deemed unfit for housing animals. One newspaper also ran a damaging story in September of that year claiming hundreds of dogs were forced to live in miserable conditions. The report said that more than 300 Labradors, Spaniels and Alsatians were locked in cruel conditions for 20 hours a day.

Members of the Veterinary Standards Inspection Team said the centre was so bad that a complete rebuild was the only viable solution. The private contractors running the Centre at that time were slammed by the local council and told to make urgent improvements. Repairs were apparently scuppered for three years because defence officials and Realm could not agree who would foot the bill. Eventually, Realm ceased to be the contractor and new kennels were purchased from another manufacturer.

Until the new accommodation was ready, dozens of dogs were boarded at private kennels at taxpayers' expense. Thankfully, the Centre's bad old days are firmly in the past. The place is immaculate and being run in a disciplined, military fashion now that the facilities are firmly back under MoD control.

No one can say there are squalid conditions at the centre now. During my visit, I peer into shiny new portable kennels that look far removed from the kind of grotty cage that Charlton Heston clambered from in *Planet of the Apes*. These new field kennels are used on exercises in the UK and also employed as homes for the dogs while they work out of smaller forward operating bases in Afghanistan. More proof, if more were needed, that these dogs are now receiving the funding they deserve as a top military asset.

A meeting with Falco and Leon rounds off our visit. These Belgian Malinois are multi-purpose military police dogs, the *creme de la creme* of the canine world. They can search for people, property, and take down would-be terrorists in the bat of an eyelid. As well as all the bite work and controlled aggression, the dogs are able to cope with peaceful members of the public on days like today. They are highly trained to be all mouth and teeth one minute and then as mild mannered as a soppy family pet the next.

It is a difficult job but one that Falco and Leon manage with consummate ease. They put on a formidable display of their bite work as several handlers don bite sleeves and allow the dogs to chomp down on their protected right arm. Falco is clearly a real professional. He is able to respond not only to verbal commands but to hand signals too. A wave of the hand by his handler, is all he needs to sit down and await further orders. It is very impressive to watch. His handler, a chatty, wavy haired and effortlessly confident corporal, is clearly well known to locals as he is on first name terms with many of the passing visitors. This is yet another indication of just how much the centre is now part of the wider Melton community.

He deserves the final word on the centre's dogs: 'A lot of the tree huggers say we shouldn't work the dogs; that it is wrong to have dogs working, but that is what they do. It's what they have always done. They love working or they just would not do it. Dogs would have disappeared long ago if they didn't work. Their skills and work ethic are why they have such a close relationship with humans and why they are still on Earth.'

Reaching down to stroke Falco, the handler explains that these particular dogs have to be able to do all sorts of work, from taking down bad guys, finding lost equipment and searching buildings to schmoozing with members of the public or dealing with law abiding demonstrators. In a split second, they have to switch from ferocious working dogs to amiable Army ambassador.

As if to emphasise his pal's point, Falco, who seconds ago had been a terrifying flash of fur and teeth as he mauled a handler's bite sleeve, ambles over to a six-year-old girl in a red jacket and camouflage trousers, rolls over and gets his tummy rubbed.

TWELVE

Old dog, new tricks

Harry gives me a furry pawed high five as soon as I walk in the door and, as I sit down, drapes himself over me as if I am part of the furniture. Harry can be forgiven for his chummy insouciance, he is, after all, one of Britain's top dogs.

Not only has he smashed insurgent bomb makers in Iraq, saving innumerable British lives, the Springer Spaniel keeps a close eye on his family in the UK when his 'daddy' goes off to battle the Taliban. The nine-year-old veteran, who retains his youthful good looks, was a supreme search dog in his day. Now though, he is enjoying an indolent, free and easy, high life in Civvy Street after being adopted by his handler.

Lance Corporal Luke Pryce was so impressed with Harry's talents, his outgoing personality and limitless enthusiasm that he fought hard to adopt him, climbing a mountain of bureaucracy and fighting through a blizzard of forms. After his victory, he sent his four legged chum back home to guard the family before going off to face the Taliban.

As I watch Harry loll about the living room floor, I can't help but think of the old adage that 'you can't teach an old dog new tricks'. Apparently, Harry still shows vestiges of his old, military life. Prone to pouncing on unsuspecting workmen, he will assail them with his highly skilled nose, probing every nook of their boiler suits and tool bags. They are forced to remove their spanners, screwdrivers and pipe cutting gear until he finds what he is after. Harry will then sit, proudly indicating that he has made a find as the gas engineer pulls out a piece of electrical insulating tape, an innocuous piece of kit but an item that is often used to build IEDs. Old habits die hard, indeed.

Harry is a top graduate of Melton Mowbray, as is his daddy Luke. Handlers can work with scores, if not hundreds, of dogs throughout their careers. As we have seen, it is not all that unusual for a soldier to work with several dogs in the course of one tour. Harry, however, was special.

As we sit in Luke's living room in his family home in Lanarkshire, just outside Glasgow, he speaks with pride of Harry's track record as a vehicle search dog in Iraq in 2005. He tells me that Harry came to him with a good reputation. 'I got paired with him back in the UK and we hit it off straight away. Dogs have their own personality, there's no doubt about it, and Harry has tremendous character. I knew I had found a pal for life. He is such a cheeky, inquisitive, warm dog, you can't help but take to him. When I saw him at work, it was as if he was teaching me. I just had to sit back and learn from his experience. He was really showing me how it was done.'

When Luke found out he was being posted to Afghanistan he knew his parents, William and Susan, were in safe hands with his best buddy there to look after them. He says: 'It was a real comfort to me out in Afghan, knowing that Harry was there with my Mum and Dad. He was great company for the family while I was serving. There were a lot of hoops to jump through to get Harry back home but there was no way I was going to give up.'

By the time Luke set off to Helmand to serve with the Royal Marines of 42 Commando in 2011, Harry was retired and fast becoming a big part of his family. On that tour, he worked with a Belgian Malinois bitch called Titch who unearthed a number of bomb making caches. 'Titch was some dog, she did around five tours back to back since she was so good. It was great to work with her. We were reunited when I came back and I saw her at a base in Germany but I couldn't wait to get home to Harry. I knew he would have been keeping an eye on the family and keeping them fully entertained with his high jinx.'

Dog handlers are a tight knit bunch; not only is Luke a close friend of Mick McConnell and Memphis, his Dad and girl-friend also work with dogs. Amber is a fellow handler in the Army while his Dad, William, works with dogs in the MOD Police. Luke and Amber were brought together by their love for working dogs. He smiles: 'It's something we have both always wanted to do. We just hit it off and have been together since.'

The couple agree that it actually helps that they work with military dogs and know both the risk and rewards of being on the frontline. Amber says: 'It is tough being apart but I know Luke is doing something he loves. I was so pleased for him when he got to re-home Harry. The dogs are more than just assets, they are comrades, best pals.'

Harry is not the perfect pet though. Leaving aside his quirky habit of occasionally switching into 'work' mode, to the cha-grin of visiting workmen, he has another major vice. 'He will eat anything and everything. He would eat himself to death if you let him,' Luke laughs. 'You wouldn't guess it to look at him, as he is slim and very healthy, but he is a glutton. In Iraq, he was searching a large van, full of nan bread, and they just could not get him out. He will stick his nose into absolutely anything. Once, my mum left a glass of sherry and when she came back he had drank it.'

Harry's life has been spent either working or in various ken-nels so he isn't used to seeing other domestic animals, such as cats. He is now making up for lost time with a passion. Luke says: 'Until he came here, Harry had never seen cats and was a bit startled at first. He got over the shock pretty quick though, and now he can't get enough of chasing them, but he is just being friendly and trying to play with them.'

Even on routine trips for a check up, Harry is known to go into search mode and scour the bemused vet's surgery for suspect items. It raises a few eyebrows but the staff and locals are getting used to Harry's idiosyncrasies. 'He is a real character and he never forgets his old job. He still has a great nose because, from time to time, he will come running with a tennis ball from God knows where. We now have this collection. He manages to find them in every nook and cranny in the house, the garden and the street.'

Luke spent hundreds of pounds on a new kennel for Harry, but it sits in the back garden unused as he never had the heart to make him sleep there. Instead, Harry's comfy bed sits underneath a picture of a handler and his dog silhouetted against the setting sun in Afghanistan. The image is emblazoned with the words of a moving poem called 'The Long Walk', a suitable place for this old veteran to have a lie and a good scratch. It reads: 'My faithful friend, I trust you so, I will follow wherever you go, you come to a stop, your tail is low, Here boy, sit!! Let's take it easy.' The lines end with the sentence 'Breath easy, we are safe at last, No British soldier will feel that blast.'

Harry, oblivious to how apt his surroundings are, munches happily on yet another chew in front of the fire. His days on the frontline are now behind him but there are still hundreds of dogs on duty 24 hours a day, serving their country. I was to meet a crack team of Britain's best trained military dogs who still have years of faithful service ahead of them at the country's most secure military base.

THIRTEEN

Nuclear hounds

My nerves start jangling as I prepare to meet the deadly elite band which is tasked with guarding enough nuclear hardware to wipe our country off the map. I am warned what to expect before entering the kennels. A senior officer tells me that most of the dogs are fine but some may get worked up as I walk through the middle of their home uninvited. He shouts above the roar: 'So please, keep in mind that they can get a bit territorial.'

My mind is racing now. If 90 per cent of the dogs are going to be okay with me, what about the other ten? I nod as Sergeant Danny Atkinson goes on: 'You might see me put my fingers up to the cage to pat the dogs as we pass through the kennel but you should keep your fingers away from the bars. Better safe than sorry.'

Venturing into the home of Britain's crack military working dogs, where many dogs are tested, but few make the grade, I receive a privileged insight into their world. Some MoD Police officers will deploy from this heavily guarded base on tours of duty to Afghanistan alongside the British Army, helping train and mentor their Afghan counterparts ahead of the drawdown which will see the return of the majority of British troops to the UK.

Sgt Atkinson reinforces what I already know, these dogs are the very top of the food chain, the apex of the military working dog world, responsible for safeguarding Britain's deadly nuclear arsenal. I am inside one of the most sensitive military bases in the UK, Her Majesty's Naval Base Clyde, known as Faslane. Nestled in the west coast of Scotland on the Gare Loch in Argyll and Bute, Faslane is one of the Royal Navy's biggest bases. It is made up of two main sites: Faslane itself and its sister site Royal Navy Armaments Depot Coulport on Loch Long.

HMNB Clyde, which perches on the loch side like a small military-industrial city, is extremely secure. Just as well since Faslane is home to the bulk of Britain's submarine service and the nation's nuclear deterrent. The latest generation of hunter-killer submarines, including the multi-billion pound Astute class subs, call this place home. More than 6500 civilians and service personnel work here. The vast complex, with its looming battleship grey buildings, cranes and windowless work sheds, is an imposing sight.

Security is tight. I have to provide my name, date of birth and nationality for security clearance before flourishing my driving licence at the gate to a series of heavily armed men behind bomb proof barriers. I then have to endure a 15 minute health and safety brief, in case of any potential nuclear accidents, before I am given the all clear to meet the dogs.

Located deep in the base at the end of a spaghetti junction of roads and roundabouts, the MoD Police dog unit sits at the centre of a sea of lethal looking razor wire and imperious CCTV towers. The unit comprises three one storey buildings: a kennel, an office and a veterinary block. There can be no doubting that I have arrived at doggy HQ given the barrage of barks and growls.

Sgt Atkinson is the top man here, a line manager, dog instructor and general jack-of-all-trades, responsible for dogs with a paw in both the military and police dog worlds. He is a young looking 45-year-old whose salt and pepper hair betrays his advancing years. Despite living in the west of Scotland for years, he retains the tell-tale hint of an accent from his native Newcastle. He grew up with two German Shepherds and once served as a RAF Police dog handler. So, dogs are in his blood.

He says: 'You will see that the dogs are like people in that they all have different personalities. 'Some will be really excited to see you, some a bit curious, others a bit territorial and wonder why you are walking through their home. We have one dog, Pico, who does the wall of death when people go into the kennels. He spins round and round and jumps off the walls. Best if you meet them and see for yourself.'

The barking reaches a crescendo when the dogs sense they are about to have a visitor. My anxiety goes up a notch when a member of the kennel staff offers me ear defenders. The dog unit is also festooned with bright yellow and black warning signs featuring a menacing image of a dog's head. These factors do not settle my nerves. Nonetheless, I take my first tentative steps into the kennels.

Dozens of German Shepherds and Belgian Malinois live here. It is their home although, I find out later, some handlers actually take their charges for doggy days out. As I am led round the kennels, with a sturdy metal grilled door always between my fragile, tender body and the dogs, I see exactly what Sgt Atkinson means about each dog having its own quirks and personality. Some bark constantly, others seem quite docile. One German Shepherd lazily wanders up to her kennel door with, what appear to be, slight bags under her eyes, as kennel worker Shona Ross offers her a treat. Shona tells me: 'She has been on night shift, that's why she is so tired. She'll go for a nap once we have left.'

Despite this dog's dopey demeanour, working in the kennels has its own dangers. Forty something Shona is shy and softly spoken when we first meet but she comes alive with enthusiasm when she describes her work. 'I am good at getting bitten,' she explains, 'I have been bitten quite a few times. It is one of these things. One of the dogs that bit me actually had neurological problems, it turned out to be a brain tumour but we didn't know that at the time. He wasn't aware at the time even though it was quite a bad bite. Dogs are like kids in that they are unpredictable. Some can be quite nervous. Over time, they come out of their shell and you see a real difference. You build a bond with them. It sounds daft but they are really pleased to see you in the morning. It brightens your day.'

The dogs, predominantly German Shepherds with the odd Belgian Malinois, are all around three feet tall, even before they stand on their hind legs to bark at me. That's more than enough dog to give intruders cause to think twice, and they are highly trained, capable of dealing with everything from Al Qaeda terrorists in bomb vests, to peace protesters, and even the odd drunk Royal Marine. As well as deterring and detaining would-be terrorists, they are trained to take out armed assailants, ignoring a hail of bullets to bring down any weapon-toting bad guys.

Shona, who lives in a small village in the countryside surrounding the base, has worked at Faslane for 18 years. She knows each of the dogs' foibles: 'Some will sit quietly and just watch while some will be up at the bars, wanting to see what is happening. Some of the dogs are what we call spinners and will just go round and round. I don't know how they don't get dizzy. Another does a wall of death. When no one is about, they are quite quiet but when someone goes near the kennels, they set each other off. One dog called Jazz even does backflips.'

After a few minutes in the kennels, I wished that I hadn't refused the ear protectors. The noise is cacophonous.

We were warned what to do if a dog gets out. There would be shouts of 'Dog loose! Dog loose!' Following the shouts

27 Photographer Lesley Martin keeps a keen eye out for a photo opportunity even during the stress of Operation Tyruna. Pic: author's own.

28 A Black Watch soldier trudges through an eye catching field of poppies. Opium from the poppies is used to fund the Taliban. Pic: Gillian Shaw.

29 Working dog Ryky – who serves with the US Army's 1st Cavalry Division – has a rest at the end of another gruelling patrol. Pic: US Army, Sgt Mary Phillips.

30 Military dog Major Butch ends her tour of duty at Bagram Airfield, Parwan province, Afghanistan in 2013. Pic: US Army, Maj Charles Patterson.

31 Military working dog Luca goes for a ride during a training exercise at Forward Operating Base Spin Boldak, Kandahar province. Pic: US Army, Sgt Michael Needham.

32 Ken Rowe and his beloved Sasha among the sand dunes of Afghanistan.
Pic: The Rowe family.

33 Ken and Sasha are among the fallen heroes commemorated at the Jigsaw memorial, near his family home outside Newcastle. Pic: Author's own.

"The Jigsaw is a metaphor
for bereavement,
the loss felt at the death
of a loved one.
It also celebrates family
and friends, standing together,
providing comfort and support
into the future."

Judith Spreadbury,
Student, North Tyneside College

34 A plaque at the Jigsaw memorial outlines the monument's meaning. It was erected in September 2000 by Sappers from the Royal Engineers. Pic: Author's own.

35 A close up of the People's Dispensary for Sick Animal (PDSA) Dickin Medal. It is the highest award an animal can receive for gallantry while serving in a conflict. Pic: Sgt Adrian Harlen. MOD/ Crown Copyright 2014.

36 US Army 1st Sgt Chris Lalonde, center, holds his military working dog Sgt Maj Fosco, while jumpmaster Kirby Rodriguez, behind them, deploys his parachute during the military's first tandem airborne jump from an altitude of 12,500 feet. Pic: US Army, Sgt Vince Vander Maarel.

37 Retired bomb busting dog Harry still holds his dignified military bearing after his years in the Army. After his exemplary service, he was adopted by his hero handler Luke Pryce. Pic: author's own.

38 An MOD Police search dog scours every inch of a car park to make sure there are no boobytrap bombs. Pic: Harland Quarrington. MOD/ Crown Copyright 2014.

39 Constable Claire Don has a hug with her dog Beila after another hard shift at Faslane Naval Base, home of Britain's nuclear deterrent. Pic: Phil Dye, Daily Record.

40 Constable Barry Fulton looks on as Harley, complete with his leonine mane of fur, makes short work of an obstacle course. Pic: Phil Dye, Daily Record.

41 Sergeant Danny Atkinson in disguise as he shows how effective a 'bite sleeve' can be as another highly trained MoD Police dog is put through its paces. Pic: Phil Dye, Daily Record.

42 A military working dog shows off its powerful bite during a display at a US base. These protection dogs are specially trained to bring down any assailant. Pic: US Air Force.

43 Paris is rewarded with some down time after clearing vehicles for explosives in Farah province, Afghanistan. Pic: US Marine Corps. Sgt Pete Thibodeau.

44 Black Watch soldiers give some TLC to a dog in an Afghan compound during a patrol. Dogs in Afghanistan are sometimes mistreated and used as guard dogs to protect family homes. Pic: Gillian Shaw.

45 VIP Cheryl Cole smiles as a military working dog goes for a paddle in the summer heat at Camp Bastion. Pic: Daily Record/Trinity Mirror.

46 A Black Watch soldier shows off the Taliban bullet which lodged in his rifle during a firefight. He wears the bullet that nearly cost him his life around his neck as a memento. Pic: Lesley Martin.

47 Soldiers scramble out of a Mastiff armoured vehicle in Kandahar, Afghanistan as they prepare for another mission into the badlands. Pic: Lesley Martin.

48 Female medics served with the Black Watch as they battled the Taliban. One female medic gave the author a crash course in emergency treatment before he embarked on Op Tyruna. Pic: Lesley Martin.

49 A row of patches on the coat of Katya, 52nd Security Forces Squadron military working dog, during a K-9 unit demonstration. Katya has been with her handler Staff Sgt Shannon Hennessy for two years.
Pic: US Air Force. Airman 1st Class Gustavo Castillo.

50 A female soldier sports the famous red hackle of 3 SCOTS, The Black Watch at Camp Roberts, Kandahar Air Field, Afghanistan. Pic: Lesley Martin.

51 Dogs have a number of roles in the Army. Conmeal, a two-year-old Irish Wolfhound is the regimental mascot of 1st Battalion Irish Guards. Pic: Sgt Ian Houlding RLC. MOD/Crown Copyright 2014.

52 Mick McConnell, his partner Lorna and Memphis are enjoying a new life together after their horrific experiences on the frontline in Afghanistan. Pic: courtesy of Mick McConnell.

the best policy is to stand still or climb the nearest available fence. Thankfully, the well-designed kennels are up to the job of keeping the dogs inside. Each animal has its own pen with a clean, concrete floor and a smaller back 'bedroom' with a comfy looking sheepskin bed blanket.

Shona says the dogs are exercised often and given a bit of free and easy downtime to unwind from the stresses and strains of their day job: 'If they didn't enjoy it or want to work, it would be very obvious. When you see the handlers put the harness on the dogs, you can see them switch on and go 'yeah, it's time to go to work now'. The dogs really love it here – it's their home. Sometimes, when you are out walking and enjoying the fresh air on a warm, summer day, you think this is a great life.'

Shona's colleague Alyson Marshall is a blonde 29-year-old who would look more at home in a beauty parlour than mucking out a busy kennel. She still loves her job after three years of cleaning dog vomit, faeces and urine. 'I arrive in the morning, get the kennels cleaned, exercise the dogs, and give them any medication they need. If they are scheduled to have any trips to the vets, we take them down there and make sure they are fine. Sometimes we take them out in the base and give them a walk on or off the lead.'

These dogs certainly don't come cheap, it costs from £3,500 to £10,000 to buy one. A further £22,000 is spent getting it fully trained and ready to go. Cheaper than one of the nearby nuclear subs maybe, but still a pricey investment.

After the head-splitting guided tour of the kennels, which were given a multi-million pound facelift a few years back, I get behind the scenes access to the nerve centre of the dog unit. The veterinary block is the hub, where the dog's health and dietary needs are assessed every day. As I walk in the door, I spot a large photographic mural of all the dogs currently working at the unit.

Their names run the gamut from the bizarre to the mundane.

Looking up at mugshots of Ambra, Cira, Pico, Adonis, Bessie, Ginge, Tacky, Harry, Jazz, Sam, Xanto, Arina, Harley and Beila, I am intrigued. Is Adonis, for example, a particularly muscular canine? Is Ginge a redhead? One of the handlers explains that the dogs are named before they arrive at Faslane.

Most of the names are quite random, with no specific connection to the dog, I am told. Names are given by their breeders, who tend to be from Eastern Europe these days. The US is also a major player in the breeding of military working dogs, and defence chiefs in the UK now look to Uncle Sam for a better breed of dog. Sgt Atkinson tells me that countries using a special kind of training called Schutzhund (German for protection dog) are now very popular when it comes to sourcing.

Schutzhund is a dog sport that was originally developed in Germany in the early 1900s for the German Shepherd. Now, the technique is used with other breeds to test whether the dogs have what it takes to thrive in military and police environments. Dog trainers use the technique to assess an animal's desire to work, its courage, intelligence, trainability, bond to the handler, perseverance and protective instinct, the key qualities of any military dog.

This form of training makes sure that British procurement teams get their hands on the best. Sgt Atkinson says: 'A lot of dogs come from the continent. The Dutch, French and Belgians are into this type of training, ensuring high quality. Sometimes the breeders mate a German Shepherd bitch with a Belgian Malinois because of its high drive. The MoD decided to bring this cross in and they have been highly successful. In the past, there were not that many German Shepherds kicking around plus the quality had suffered because a lot of the breeders had gone down the show line. The dogs may look good, but they aren't that great, physically, for a police dog. Many had hip dysplasia issues and other ailments.'

140

This veterinary facility boasts a dazzling selection of mod cons including a laundry for the dog's towels, sheepskin bedding and a shower room complete with special doggy hairdryer. There is even a 'retirement room', sporting pictures of old dogs that have done their bit and are now enjoying their twilight years. I am told that when one of the dogs passed away his handler had him cremated so that he could keep the ashes.

So much attention to detail is on display here. Each dog has its own 'enrichment toy', a large ball made of strong plastic, which is filled with treats so the dog has to work out how to get at them. The busiest part of the facility, the expansive food preparation area, is filled with gleaming bins of dried pellets. Unappetising as it looks and smells, this concoction is rocket fuel for dogs, helping them get through a gruelling day of duties.

I am gobsmacked at the immaculate surroundings and the sheer amount of food. It must be a logistical nightmare keeping these ravenous working dogs fed and watered. According to the MoD's own guidelines, the amount of food given to dogs depends on a number of factors including 'temperament, work rate and environment'. Small dogs weighing under 20 kilogrammes receive 250 to 450 grammes of dry food a day while average sized get 400 to 600 grammes. Bigger dogs, such as the German Shepherds, receive up to 850 grammes of food.

Dogs here are fed on Eukanuba, a type of round, brown pellet that smells rather fishy to my untrained nose. Shona jokingly offers me a handful of the nutritious pebbles saying they taste quite good but I politely decline, thinking they resemble animal droppings.

Dogs even have an agility area where they can go for a well-earned stretch. More often than not though, they just want to curl up and get comfy on Shona's lap.

Each dog is given a regular health check up in the gleaming

and well equipped veterinary room, where vets check their weight daily. If a dog is losing weight, it can indicate a health problem while a sudden weight gain might suggest that the animal is sluggish and not burning off enough calories while exercising.

Next, we are off to see the dogs being put through their paces. We leave the quiet sanctity of the veterinary block to go to the doggy assault course which Pico, Adonis and their kennel mates have to pass to get their military police dog licences, piling into vans to do so. The need to drive to the training ground re-emphasises yet again the sheer scale of the base. It resembles a thriving naval city perched on the banks of the loch.

Hidden among the mysterious looking hangars and boat sheds is the dog's proving ground, where tricky looking obstacles are flanked on all sides by an eight foot high fence to deter over-exuberant runaways. I am quietly warned that the dog I am about to meet is an excellent military working dog but I must avoid getting too close.

Harley caught my eye earlier in the kennels as he is the shaggiest looking of all the German Shepherds. Very protective of his handler, to put it mildly, he doesn't like strangers. His long sable coat, dotted black, gold and brown, is a picture of good health and vitality, testament to the great work of the kennel staff. Sadly, it has not always been this way for Harley.

He came to Faslane from the Defence Animal Centre in Melton Mowbray after the Battersea Dogs Home. It is hard to trace the exact origins of each dog but his new colleagues believe he was abused as a pup by his owners before being dumped. Harley, however, is a real rags to riches story. Despite his grim start in life, he is now established as one of the MoD Police's finest, whose enthusiasm and natural drive always shine through.

He has proved himself time and time again coping with all

sorts of duties from herding belligerent protesters to finding lost property. Sporting an impressive leonine mane, Harley ambles onto the training area like a gladiator entering the arena, accompanied by his beloved handler Constable Barry Fulton. He is incredibly attached to Constable Fulton which may explain why he gets upset if anyone else gets too close.

I watch, at a suitably safe distance, as Harley makes mincemeat of daunting obstacles that would strain lesser dogs. Protecting Britain's nuclear arsenal, taking down gun toting fanatics and managing threatening crowds is all in a day's work for him, so the course was easy pickings. He vaults around it, gambolling over the three foot hurdle before sprinting through the twelve foot tunnel, clearing the long jump and see saw, and ending with a triumphant gallop over the wooden A-frame.

Once Harley is safely in the back of the dog van I chat to Constable Fulton. He explains that Harley's mistreatment at the hands of his civilian owners had cast a long shadow. 'It is sometimes quite hard to trace the exact details of the dog's life before he or she came to us but we think Harley may have been mistreated. When someone walks in the kennels, the other dogs get all excited but he tends to cower away and look nervous.'

Harley came to Faslane from Battersea Dogs Home about six years ago: 'He was handed in by a couple that had separated and neither wanted to take responsibility. So I got him when he was 14 months. He is fine when he's working but, personality wise, you don't want to get anywhere near if I am not there. He has got a tendency just to fly without any sort of warning. He is very handler protective. If someone comes into my personal space, he will go for them. It's possibly a hangover from his previous life. I managed to do a bit of digging and found out that he was from a broken home. I think he has possibly bitten someone in the past. You see him in the kennel, while all the rest of the dogs are barking and spinning around, he cowers down really low. I know he is like that so it is not a problem.'

Dog lover Constable Fulton's eight years of experience in this job and his stocky, well-built frame are enough to keep Harley in check. He says: 'He is a great all round dog. When he's working, he switches on to what he is doing. It's only if someone takes me by surprise, he will go to the end of the lead to try and get to them. That can be a good thing if you are sent to deal with half a dozen blokes. He caught a German chap, who was a Quaker, who got through the fence a couple of years back. From the time of the alarm going off to me going out with Harley and finding him in the bushes was about 11 minutes. He was pretty quick to get him.'

Harley has proved to be a flexible, invaluable member of the team despite his unhappy upbringing. His abilities to track and search are second to none. He gets a chance to put them to good use regularly as dogs and handlers work closely with the local civilian police.

Constable Fulton explains: 'I was recently sent up to a housing estate after they received a call. A woman had lost her car and house keys at 4 in the morning. Harley picked up the woman's scent on the keys and found them. The lady was chuffed. He is a brilliant dog to work with. It's great that he has managed to go from Battersea to here where he is such a valuable member of the team.'

After our chat, Sgt Atkinson and his team of handlers take me to the base's jetty to show me the power, agility and obedience of Harley and his comrades. Several minesweepers are docked here so the sailors are in for a good show, but woe betide any of them that blunders down the gangplank. Sgt Atkinson dons what appears to be a bulky, beige toned desert camouflage jacket which looks as if it has seen better days. I stand well back among the ropes and other naval detritus at the side of the jetty as Harley gears up to show how he deals with any interlopers.

Sgt Atkinson puts on a performance fit for the Oscars as he plays the role of a would-be attacker. He waves his arms in the air, shouting a stream of bloodcurdling oaths at the top of his voice as a number of bemused sailors strain to get a better look from the deck of their ship. His threatening display continues after Constable Fulton issues a warning to stop or he will release his dog. Right on cue, Harley is let off his leash and rockets along the jetty.

Within seconds, he catches up with Sgt Atkinson, leaps through the air and sinks his teeth into the reinforced bite sleeve hidden in the camouflage jacket. With a firm grip on the sleeve, Harley thrashes from side to side as his teeth work their way into the thick, jute padding of the sleeve. Another handler tells me that, far from finding this type of work difficult or painful, the dogs actually love it and would do it all day given half a chance. It is every dog's dream.

Harley and his chums are also trained in what's known in the trade as the 'stand off'. This drill means that if Harley is bearing down on a bad guy who suddenly sees the error of his ways and gives up, Harley will pull off and not launch himself at him. The dogs have to show completely controlled aggression. A dog who gets too worked up and can't master his emotions will not make the grade in this job. German Shepherd Beila is brought in to demonstrate how these dogs can go from attack mode to placid in seconds.

His handler, Constable Claire Don, brings Beila onto the jetty, looking for all the world like a family pet out for a stroll. Chatting earlier, Constable Don explained how she had worked in a number of jobs, from supermarket manager to shop assistant, before ending up in her dream job as a dog handler. 'I have been in the job for about five years and I love it. I trust Beila 100 percent. He can be boisterous, but also very chilled. It is very easy to read how he is feeling. He is great for the job and I definitely feel safer with him around. He is a great deterrent.'

With her slim build, glasses and well-tended russet hair, Constable Don looks nothing like the stereotypical image of a military policewoman. She does have, however, a commanding presence and a pistol when on duty with Beila. As they stroll along the jetty, Sgt Atkinson, again in his guise as a villain, springs from the storage containers beside the walkway and starts gesticulating before going into full blown, bad guy mode.

After he is warned to cease and desist, Beila is let off the leash and given the command to do his stuff. He bolts along the walkway in silence until, just inches from his target, Constable Don lets out a high pitched squeal: 'Sttttooooooooooooppp! Noooo!!!' Her piercing, distinctly female shout nearly knocks me off my feet but it has the desired effect on Beila who stops dead in his tracks, turns and awaits further commands. A textbook manoeuvre and testament to these dogs' incredible obedience, focus and mental strength.

Beila can switch from fearsome attacker to attentive puppy on command; amazing to watch. Constable Don jokes: 'Sometimes it pays to have a feminine, higher pitched voice as it certainly gets the dogs attention.' And mine, if my frayed nerves are anything to go by.

Now that I have seen them in action, I have little doubt that Harley, Beila and the rest of the dogs are part of one of the most adaptable forces in the military world. They have to be able to search for people and property and swoop on terrorists, while still being at home at the local fayre being patted by small kids.

The MoD's elite police dog unit employs around 300 fully trained police dogs and handlers working at military sites around the UK. This makes the force the biggest user of police dogs in the country. Most of the animals here at Faslane are general purpose police dogs, like Harley, trained to search for evidence, people and to restrain 'ne'er do wells'. Sourced and trained by the Defence Animal Centre in Melton Mowbray, they are the only police dog teams in the UK to carry out high risk explosives searches.

I'm eager to meet one of the cuddlier and more approachable arms and explosive search dogs after my arms' length meeting with Harley and his chums. Many are trained in specialised areas such as tactical firearms support, drugs detection or vehicle search. Tactical firearms support dogs are deployed as a 'less than lethal' option at any serious incident while arms and explosive search dogs, such as the one I now meet, a cuddly jet black crossbreed called Toby, are housed with their handlers at home and quickly become part of the family.

Toby can find everything from small pistols to massive bomb making caches. According to the MoD, arms and explosive dogs are a 'high profile, effective deterrent used as a pro-active response to the threat from terrorist activity', but when I catch sight of Toby, he seems more like a good natured family pet rather than a steely eyed military wonder dog. He is also determined to lick me to death. Toby's long hair is soaked by the ubiquitous west coast of Scotland drizzle but it doesn't dampen his enthusiasm to see me. He is completely overjoyed to get so much attention on what, to him, seems like a normal working day.

He looks like a big, soppy mongrel but once his harness is put on, he drops his head and snaps seamlessly into working mode. His handler PC Martin Preston says: 'Toby is a great worker. Once the harness goes on, he knows the score and is very professional. It's just like he switches on and knows immediately what is required.'

A realistic looking starter pistol is hidden on the jetty

underneath a rusting metal drain cover while Toby is distracted by his 'daddy' PC Preston. Then Toby is brought back to the end of the jetty and with a sweep of his handler's hand and the command to search. He's off! His nose is twitching like mad at the olfactory overload in front of him: the scent of several humans, the acrid earthy pong of diesel and oil, even the fishy tang of mussels clinging to the legs of the jetty.

Toby scours every inch of the walkway, weaving from side to side. He moves quickly and it isn't long before he is on to something. With his tail waggling in every direction, Toby is the epitome of the word 'focus'. Within a few feet of the weapon, his body language changes and, as he gets closer, he stares at the gun and goes down on his haunches. This is the sign that he has made a find. In days gone by, dogs were trained to bark or give some other signal but, to my mind, this signal is unmistakable.

None of the military dogs I encounter bark to signal a find as the noise could also give the dog team's position away. Barking would be a particularly risky manoeuvre in the context of Afghanistan, where the Taliban could be lurking unseen in the surrounding countryside.

Once Toby pinpoints the gun, PC Preston launches his rubber toy near where he found the weapon, creating the impression in Toby's mind that the toy just appears like 'magic'. Unlike the fiercer looking German Shepherds and Belgian Malinois, Toby and the base's other search dogs stay at home with their handlers. PC Preston tells me: 'He is just like a member of the family. He loves coming to work. He is not a pedigree or anything like that but he is very effective when it comes to finding weapons. I tell people he is a thing, but a good looking thing! These dogs are a wonderful addition to our armoury. They pick out the scent of the weapon and then signal to their handler that they have made a find by sitting or lying down. For them, it's all just a game and they really love their job.

Their reward is the appreciation of their handler and some affection.'

After braving the cold and drizzle for several hours, we retire to Sgt Atkinson's cosy office to discuss his dogs. Over a reviving cup of sugary tea, he mentions a remarkable dog who was out pounding the beat. German Shepherd Ony has an impressive record. After a stint at the Defence Animal Centre, she served in Iraq with the British Army's elite Special Air Service or SAS. Sgt Atkinson, who has been with the Faslane dog unit for eight years after spells with the RAF police and the civil nuclear constabulary, says that such dogs are at the apex of the military dog world.

'They are pretty much up there,' he gestures with his hand over his head, 'I would say that the MoD Police gives dogs some of the highest levels of training. Our standards are extremely high. Ony is a prime example, she is an Eastern European dog who started off with the UK's Special Forces, hunting insurgents among reed beds in Iraq.'

He adds: 'For some reason, she didn't meet all their criteria and she was transferred. We never got to know why she didn't make the full grade with the SAS but she has turned out to be one of the best dogs we have had. Obviously, the standard that Special Forces are looking for is extremely high. That's our good fortune.'

Some of the dogs here have even saved the lives of soldiers who got lost on exercise in the wild countryside around the base. Dogs are occasionally sent to find and rescue soldiers who have failed to turn up at a rendezvous point. These dogs can search for people in a variety of terrains, whether woodland, open areas or urban areas.

On a long leash and a harness, Harley, Ony and the rest of the unit are trained in old MoD housing units in a nearby village. It is in these small houses, once used to house sailors and their families, that the dogs' tracking skills are finely honed.

Their ability to search and find people is constantly tested in real life scenarios.

Sgt Atkinson tells me of one such incident, involving a car crash in the early hours of the morning: 'The car was abandoned when Pico and his handler went to deal with the call. The handler cast Pico around the vehicle and he eventually pulled off 150 yards down the road where they found two Polish immigrants who had debussed from the vehicle as they were drunk as skunks. They had gone to ground because they knew they had a lot to drink. Pico picked up the track very quickly and found them hiding in the bushes.'

This unit's close liaison with the local civilian police often gets the dogs involved in bizarre cases, such as catching one of the country's daftest crooks. Sgt Atkinson stifles a laugh as he elaborates. 'We had a handler recently who was working with Police Scotland officers after a housebreaking in the posh houses in the local town of Helensburgh. The culprit had taken all the gear out of the house but didn't notice that his phone had fallen out of his pocket. The dog found the phone very quickly. An officer examined it, found it held a contact called 'mum' and rang the number. He said 'Hi, who does this phone belong to?' The mum says 'Johnny, is that you?' The officer says 'Johnny who?' and she replies, let's say 'Johnny Smith'. Now this guy was a known delinquent in the town. He had left the house with a couple of thousand pounds worth of gear but left his phone at the scene. Let's just say, he wasn't the brightest criminal in the world.'

These dogs have to be the best in the business so, inevitably, many recruits fail to meet the grade. In a historic move in July 2010, the MoD found a novel solution to the problem of finding suitable trainee working dogs. They began to breed their own pups. Proud mum Willow, a Springer Spaniel, gave birth to twelve puppies, the first to be born at Her Majesty's

Naval Base Devonport. Her bundles of joy were part of the new programme to breed their own recruits, guaranteeing that the pups have the right breeding to meet the demands of the job. MoD police chiefs still buy in dogs but this move marked a major expansion for the dog unit.

At Faslane, Sgt Atkinson agrees that the future is bright, even in these troubled financial times: 'The dog section is biggest it has ever been. The training and the dogs are improving all the time. Say there was an incident when some service member used a firearm within the base, or a civilian came into base with a firearm, our dogs are trained to deal with that situation and will engage with someone firing a weapon at them. They will take on someone with a firearm. These dogs have to be able to show totally controlled aggression. We can deploy to a firearms incident and if the person gives up or drops the firearm and does a runner, the handler can use the dog to stop them there.'

It's not only the odd dog that fails to make the grade, but would-be handlers can also fall by the wayside. Sgt Atkinson reveals that not everyone has the stomach to be a good dog handler. 'We have 18 dogs here and 30 plus dogs at the adjoining Coulport naval base as there is more ground to cover. You have to do two years' probation as a police officer before coming into the dog unit. If you can't go into a kennel full of dog crap and pee and clean it out, then you are not going to be a dog handler. It sounds so basic but you would be surprised by the amount of people that think they love dogs because they have seen a bit of the training and the freedom that handlers get, but then when you say 'clean that muck up' they say 'whoa I can't do that'.

'There is a two week assessment before they begin training. The only way we can work with our cousins in the County forces is if we have the police dog licence, with the same training levels and intensity as our colleagues.'

He says that even some RAF and Army dogs are not up to the same standards as the crack canines on patrol at Faslane. He says: 'Some military dogs can work in an operational sense in Afghanistan or within military establishments in the UK but some of them can't go outside the fence and work in a civilian environment. Dogs have to interact with children one moment, then stand off and face service personnel that are drunk or violent or, if they are working in Civvy Street, face a couple of thugs that want to take the world on. We also need dogs that can be passive when something like a peace protest is going on.'

Hundreds of warships and submarines move in and out of Faslane every year, making it one of the busiest naval ports in the UK. So, dogs here have to cope with this maritime environment as a potential threat could lurk anywhere. Dogs are trained to search destroyers, frigates and submarines. They work closely with specialist firearms teams to 'neutralise' any intruder on a boat or member of service personnel who has gone 'rogue'.

Searching ships is broadly similar in technique to the methods used by dogs to search building, but Sgt Atkinson says that this naval environment has its own risks. 'Ships are difficult because of their nature. They have a lot more hazards to contend with – oil, electrical gear or chemicals. The dogs have special harnesses and handlers will lift them up or down from the recesses of the boat. If it's really deep, they have a piece of equipment which is a bit like a rope access harness. They get clipped into that and pulleyed down. An armed officer at the bottom will unclip them and move them on. We cover lorries, coaches, trains, just to give them a different perspective.'

More than £3.5 million is being lavished on the kennels and associated facilities at Faslane and Coulport to make sure these dogs live in the lap of luxury when they are not out pounding the beat and serving their country. Off duty dogs must get at least one hour's exercise every 24 hours, according to the dog unit's strictly observed guidelines. Animal lovers can rest assured that they dogs are well looked after but, sooner or later, the time comes when they dogs have to hang up their leash and retire.

When dogs retire, at roughly the age of nine years, handlers have the chance to adopt their buddy. Each case is judged on its own merits. There is no avoiding the sad truth that some dogs, due to their temperament, are just not suitable to move into a normal family home. Sgt Atkinson explains: 'If we deem their temperament is good enough for a home environment then the handler will get the chance to adopt his or her dog.' Motioning towards the kennels opposite his office, he continues: 'If the handlers were in a position to retire the dogs, there are a lot of dogs in there that could easily go home with them. We have to be very careful. Handlers sign disclaimers and they have to have insurance, if anything happens it's down to them. We haven't had any issues at all – so far.'

As we walk outside, Harley is leaping from the dog van as he goes out on patrol and I use the lull in proceedings to grab a quick word with Constable Fulton. How Harley will fare when he comes to retirement age? His rocky upbringing before he came here, and his extreme protectiveness towards his handler, makes him an unlikely, if not impossible, prospect.

Constable Fulton looks pensive behind his square shaped glasses as he ponders his dedicated pal's fate. They have worked together for six years; so, will he take him home at the end of his working life? 'I have four kids and I would never forgive myself if anything happened', he tells me, 'I would dearly love to take him home but if I'm here at work, there is no-one at home to deal with him. He will go back down south and be used for training. I have always had dogs, but working with Harley has been great. He is quite a character. He has shown me just how much there is in this job that interests me.'

So, Harley will, one day, help to train a new generation back where his military career started all those years ago at the Defence Animal Centre in Melton Mowbray. At eight-years-old, he is a grizzled veteran, and is entering his twilight years as a working dog at Faslane. His fluffy mane is easy to spot as he saunters off, oblivious to the drizzle gusting in from the loch. He gets one last, quick pet behind the ear before he sets off around the base with his 'daddy', looking completely unfazed as a massive, black submarine glides by on the loch's inky waters, the crew standing silently to attention on deck.

FOURTEEN

Battling on

Mick finds out the hard way that adopting a military working dog is not always easy, even if he is your best pal. Would-be adoptees, like Mick, have to negotiate a maze of red tape and form filling. Mick fills out pages of application forms and makes dozens of phone calls. It's a lengthy process, but this is a true labour of love.

All the time, he wonders if his boy will even recognise him. Maybe their relationship will not be the same after the trauma of the IED blast. The clock is ticking and he doesn't even know if Memphis will recognise him or want to have anything to do with him. The thought makes him feel even more nauseous than the painkillers he gets from the doctors. Mick's fight to get back on his feet, literally and metaphorically, is intricately tied to his battle to get Memphis back. He will go to any lengths but, as his experience on the frontline shows, Mick is a fighter in every sense of the word.

He blots out the pain from his injuries to plough through sheaves of documents requesting details about his background, his family, his relationship with the dog and so on. Luckily, handlers are first in line when it comes to adoption, but that's no guarantee that he will ultimately be successful.

Prospective adoption candidates are interviewed to determine their expectations and experience and the living environment for the dog. Demand for some retired military dogs is high, so families may wait from two months to a year to get their new pet. As we have seen, sadly, some types of military dogs will never be deemed suitable.

Ages of retired, adopted dogs may vary. Some may be between eight and 12 years old, having served one or more operational tour. Others, who perhaps didn't make it through basic training, may be as young as two to four-years-old.

Injured veterans like Mick face a double battle. He, like thousands of others, must come to terms with life changing injuries. Life truly will never be the same again. Mick also faces the gut wrenching fact that he can never again serve on the frontline. Amid all of this physical and mental turmoil, he is desperately fighting to get his four legged comrade back.

In the US, the world's biggest employer of military working dogs, Mick knows that first priority for adoption of military working dogs is often offered to the handler, then to police forces and finally to civilian families. Does the same process apply in the UK, he wonders? Approximately 300 dogs each year are adopted out from the military to private homes in the US while some 100 eligible former military working dogs are reassigned to law enforcement agencies. Without warning, as Mick returns from yet another bout of gruelling physiotherapy at Headley Court, he gets a phone call with the answer to his question.

FIFTEEN

Ultimate sacrifice

Walking in front of a snaking patrol of infanteers, sniffing out danger, scouring every inch of the terrain, is a nerve jangling daily routine for dogs and handlers in Afghanistan. Pushed to the limits in their relentless mission to outwit the Taliban, two British dog teams have sadly been killed.

Ken Rowe and his dog Sasha were the first, both killed in action in 2008. Ken's pal, fellow soldier Liam Tasker and his Spaniel, Theo, died in combat three years later. Their tragic deaths have cast a long shadow.

On a crisp morning with jagged patches of frost dotting the pavements, I am honoured to meet Ken Rowe's family. Remembrance Day has just passed, when the nation showed its respect for the fallen. I didn't choose the date especially, but it adds a certain poignancy to my arrival at a two storey house in a very respectable Tyneside suburb.

Once I get out of my car, I know immediately that I am in the right place. Two cars in the driveway sport large poppies in their front grills as well as on their windscreens. Help for Heroes stickers are festooned across the rear windows. The living room window also displays a blood red poppy, and a closer look reveals a plaque with dog tags inscribed with the name, Lance Corporal Kenneth Rowe. I have arrived.

It is now three years since he was killed alongside Sasha. Ken was one of the dog handlers who inspired me to find out more about these extraordinary working dogs. He was the first dog handler I read about after I first saw, and then became fascinated by, the military working dog teams in Helmand Province. His story would have been remarkable anyway but, sadly, he won a place in history as the first British dog handler to die in Afghanistan.

Ken and Liam both died alongside their dogs, Ken with Sasha and Liam with Theo. Ken and Liam were good pals. So much so that, after Ken was killed, Liam helped to carry his coffin. He also designed a new entrance to the kennels at Camp Bastion in honour of his pal, kennels that were named Rowe Lines in his memory. The hand carved, wooden facade stills stands today; now with Liam's name under Ken's, and Theo's directly under Sasha's. In death, both men's families are connected. Both know the pain of losing a dog handler son on the frontline.

Ken may have passed away years ago but when I meet his mum, Lyn, and dad, Kenneth senior, his presence still fills the family home.

As I am welcomed into the bright, semi-detached house which nestles midway between the rolling fields of Northumbria and the bustle of Newcastle, I can't help but notice that reminders of Ken are everywhere. My eyes roam across his medals and photographs lining the walls, his dog tags mounted and sitting in the window, and statues and plaques in his honour across the hallway. The house retains a vibrant, lived in, homely feel and is far from being a mausoleum.

In the front living room I am greeted by his auburn haired daughter, Hannah. At three-years-old she already closely resembles her dad. Eager to get a crafty glance at the stranger, she peeks at me from behind a chair. It feels as though Ken will walk back in the door at any time, throw off his kit bag and slump in front of the television for some well-earned rest and recuperation.

His pet turtle, Trevor, gamely nudges my feet as I sit on the black leather sofa. Trevor is a living, breathing testament to Ken's deep love of animals and his lifelong dream of working with them. Ken always planned for some such job, flirting with the idea of becoming a police dog handler before eventually joining the Army. His mum Lyn explains: 'Kenneth got Trevor before his tour started. He said to me: "Mum can you look after him and I will pick him up when I get back?" I sighed and thought "Ok, leave him, who else is going to look after him?" Now, look at the size of him! Trevor the turtle has a walk every day. If he hasn't had his walk at a certain time, he bangs the glass or moves it and tries to get out himself. We sometimes hear a thud when he has let himself out. His vivarium is quite a height so you can hear him throw himself on the floor kamikaze style. I thought looking after Trevor was going to be a short term six month thing . . .'

Her words hang in the air, heavy with emotion. Lyn assures me that Ken loved his Army job to the end. As she speaks, she pushes aside her jet black hair to reveal features which bear a notable resemblance to her son's. 'We have always had family pets and dogs in the family. Kenneth always loved dogs especially,' she says, 'He always going on as a child saying "Can I have a dog, can I?" We had rabbits, hamsters, gerbils, a cat, you name it. He really loved his work, every picture we have with him with the dogs, just full of smiles.'

Lyn clears the table to make way for her laptop which she hooks to the living room television, so we can better look through family snaps of Ken and Sasha at home and in Afghanistan.

With her well coiffeured hair, designer clothes, delicate gold earrings and small crucifix around her neck, Lyn looks like an elegant, well-heeled businesswoman. She speaks with the merest hint of her native Newcastle. Lyn gave up her office job after 34 years as she struggled to come to terms with the loss of her son. 'I couldn't get through a day without breaking down, but sometimes the staff would get as upset and I would be the one who had to console them.'

As digital images pop up on the TV screen, little Hannah plucks up the courage to speak to me: 'It's my daddy, Kenneth,' she shouts, transfixed by a picture of Ken in uniform. Lyn scrolls through the photos, giving me a running commentary on their significance. Like many handlers, Ken worked with a number of highly trained dogs throughout his career.

She says: 'Kenneth did a six month tour in Northern Ireland. The dog pictured here is Odie. He managed to get him rehoused. One weekend he came home from Northern Ireland and started trying to find him a new home. Odie was ready to come out of the army and retire. Kenneth found a couple in a farm near Bedlington who were willing to take him on. He introduced them and as far as we know he is still happy there.'

Judging by the pictures, Ken was a very active person and a sports fan. His tall, dark and handsome physique made him a popular figure with ladies on the streets of his home town of Newcastle. In the images, he looks like a younger, military version of Spanish singer Julio Iglesias with his sallow skin, chocolate brown eyes and cheeky smile. Hannah has inherited his exuberance and takes to climbing the sofa as we look through the images, knocking my voice recorder to the floor a few times as she scrambles up Lyn's chair, mountaineer style, to get a better look.

Lyn continues: 'This dog is called Jackdaw, Kenneth had different dogs for different activities, such as tracking. They don't like to call them sniffer dogs because they all sniff. He was all solid, bullish, and his head was about the same size as Kenneth's.'

As we study the images on the screen, Lyn says: 'You can see from his face that he loved what he did.' Her voice wavers before she breaks down into soft sobs. 'I promised I wasn't going to get upset,' she says.

I feel guilty for asking her to revisit these memories of her son, but she seems glad of the chance to talk about Ken. 'He was very much a sportsman as well, even at school he did all sorts of sports: tennis, badminton, football, rugby, cricket, squash, golf, we still have his golf clubs. He loved cross country; he actually ran for his school. He played football for Melton Town while he was at the Defence Animal Centre.'

After his death, Ken's personal belongings, including his laptop computer, were returned to his family. 'When we got his laptop back, the Army told us it was beyond repair. It was full of dust and sand. They were saying "you won't be able to get anything off it". The army screens laptops like this, to make sure there is nothing relating to intelligence matters on there. As it happened, we did manage to get it repaired and we got loads of pictures off it. He loved the job, we have even kept his handwritten training manuals.'

Lyn reveals that Ken was well on the way to making it to the top flight of dog trainers. She says: 'He got to Class Two as a trainer and would have gone on to Class One. We have spoken to Frank, his warrant officer and chief trainer down at Melton, who said Ken had the greatest aspirations and he knows he would have gone far. He had progressed quickly – he did arms and explosive search, vehicle search, all that. It was arms and explosives search he ended up specialising in. He was put in for a corporal stripe twice but got knocked back because he hadn't been in the army long enough. He was a lance corporal and he was ready for his corporal stripe in the January but unfortunately didn't make that.'

Lyn dabs her eyes as she explains that Ken had a narrow escape just months before he died. He was travelling in a Land

Rover with a dog called Diesel when the vehicle was blown up by a roadside bomb. Lyn says: 'In April, his vehicle was blown to bits and Diesel his original dog was returned home. Diesel was slightly injured. Ken was in hospital for a while but even then he was asking to get back on the frontline. After the IED blast, he told his officer "I'm fine sir can I just go back to the front?"'

The images show Ken with a number of dogs: Sasha, Irwin, Diesel. Even when he lies on the ground after another gruelling patrol alongside Sasha, whose fur is damp with sweat, they both look content. 'He had so many dogs to be honest,' Lyn says, 'it's only now that you start getting familiar with them.'

Each year, the family makes a pilgrimage to the National Arboretum, the nation's 'centre of remembrance' in Alrewas, Staffordshire, to lay a wreath to mark the anniversary of Ken's death. Lyn says: 'On the second anniversary, some of his squadron were in Bosnia and they climbed a mountain near Sarajevo to lay a marble plaque. They took turns carrying it. They told us that they would like to think if anyone goes up the mountain, they will see the stone, look his name up online and find out why he is remembered there. It's something his mates wanted to do for him. They placed the memorial near Sarajevo as that's where they were stationed at the time.'

Just a mile or two from their home, another memorial, the Jigsaw Memorial, in the shape of a jigsaw puzzle with missing pieces to symbolise lost loved ones, has become the focus of their grief.

Lyn says: 'The Jigsaw Memorial is a tribute to the fallen since World War Two. There's a chap commemorated there who fell in the Falklands, then Kenneth. It is supposed to represent members of the family together, and the missing pieces of the people who are no longer there. There is also Rowe Lines at Camp Bastion where Liam Tasker redesigned the kennels, and a memorial wall brought back from Basra. It was taken down stone by stone and rebuilt at the Arboretum. We have asked that when the army pulls out of Afghanistan, they can bring back the frontage from Rowe Lines and place it either at the military working dog regiment or the Arboretum itself, as it would be a fitting tribute to Liam and Kenneth.'

Our conversation has been light hearted enough, considering the subject, but becomes more sombre when I ask about the night of Ken's death. Lyn's face drops as she relives the experience. She had a premonition, perhaps a mother's uncanny instinct, that something was wrong.

'A man came to the door at about ten to two in the morning. As it happened, I had had a very restless night; I just knew something was wrong. I was lying awake and I heard the car pull up. I thought it was unusual at that time. I heard footsteps coming down the path and the awful knock on the door. When I went downstairs, the man put his badge against the window. It was warm so I had the windows open, I heard him say: "Are you Mrs Rowe, can you open the door please?" I said no. When I think about it now, it was silly of me, I would have had to let him in. I said no because I knew what he had come to tell me . . . and I didn't want to know.'

Lyn's expression dissolves in tears, leaving me feeling guilty for provoking her anguish. Ken was killed in action on July 24, 2008. He had volunteered to stay longer on the frontline and died the day after he should have returned home. After she composes herself and wipes her cheeks, she goes on: 'Eventually my husband had to get up because I think I had him standing at the door for ten minutes and wouldn't let him in. I told him I can't because if I let you in, you will tell me.'

Amid the grief, we still have the occasional lighter moment as we look through the Rowe family snaps. One image shows Ken covered in sand and looking rather sorry for himself. Lyn laughs: 'He said he felt like a bit of Kentucky Fried Chicken in this one. They were in Afghanistan and high winds kicked in while they were out in the desert. He thought they all looked like something from KFC, as if they were all coated in breadcrumbs.'

Another picture shows Danish soldier Martin Kristiansen who was killed with his dog after Ken's death. The 33-year-old dog handler lost his life and four other soldiers were wounded when their armoured personnel carrier was hit by an IED near Camp Budwan, Helmand. Lyn explains: 'We stumbled across this picture online. It's just that this cuts across nationalities. Ken would often work with the Danes to cross reference their training. You don't really get to hear what happens with the coalition forces from other countries. To be honest, Kenneth thought the Americans were a bit brash, he definitely preferred to work with the Danish any time.'

Our conversation meanders but, almost inevitably, keeps returning to the time of Ken's death. Every serviceman and woman is encouraged to write a last letter to their family which will be opened only in the event of their death. These so-called 'death letters' are intensely private, voicing intimate thoughts that the soldier will never get a chance to say in person.

'Kenneth's death letter says "for the eyes of Lyn Rowe only",' she says. 'I read it to the family. In the letter, he mentions all the family one by one, gives them their little tributes and says his thank yous. He was very much a family person. He says whatever you do, you will achieve it so stick at it. That's the kind of thing he would always say and the kind of person he was.'

Hundreds of mourners gathered at St Bartholomew's Church in Newcastle, for Ken's funeral service in August 2008. His coffin was carried into the church as the rock ballad 'More Than Words' by the band Extreme was played.

Remembrance Day is always an emotional time with the Rowe family. Lyn tells me: 'On Armistice day, we go up to the

Jigsaw Memorial, for our local service. Kenneth has a plaque there. We come from a well-known family, my mum, dad and I, so when it happened people knew the family anyway. We were contacted by a retired Army major who told us what the local council were going to do in Kenneth's memory. We didn't have to make a request. A lot of the veterans knew my mum and dad so they also knew the history behind Kenneth. I just thank God that my mum and dad aren't alive because it would have been heartbreaking for them. I know how I feel but I know how badly they would have felt.'

Lyn and Kenneth senior have now formed a bond with Liam Tasker's family, especially his mum, Jane Duffy. For both families, it is a bond they wish they never had, formed through grief and tragedy.

Adding a another layer of sadness, grief for Ken is accompanied by a lingering sense of disappointment, with Lyn feeling that Ken's death has been overshadowed. She says: 'I do feel as if we have been forgotten. At the time when Kenneth died with Sasha, we were told that the Army didn't want to blow it all up in the news because the animal rights activists would have created Holy Hell at the thought of using animals out there and animals having died. The army seemed to think that activists would kick off because we were forcing animals out there to do a job. We were told, more or less, to keep it low key. We were told you won't hear much recognition of it. It will be mentioned on the news, it will say he died with his dog but we will leave it at that. Afterwards we heard about the "Millie" military awards and other dog awards and nothing like that was raised with us, because we were told 'you have got to keep it quiet'.

This perceived lack of recognition of Ken and Sasha's supreme sacrifice is a lingering source of distress, Lyn confesses. 'We actually stewed on that a little bit because we thought that, yes, Kenneth has died with his dog. Give him some recognition. I thought, isn't it different yet, after three years, so now they couild give Liam that recognition. Yet we were told to keep it hush hush. They said "keep quiet, we know what has happened, we know how good he was and how he volunteered to go back on the front-line".'

Lyn shakes her head as she remembers the last words she ever spoke to her dear son: 'What were the last words I said to him? "Don't be so bloody clever as to volunteer for anything ok?" "Ok mum", he replied.'

Ken senior is an imposing older man, well over six feet tall. He looks to be in his fifties but still has a full head of greying hair. He has been a man of few words today as Lyn has been talking me through the family album. However, he kindly offers to drive me to the Jigsaw Memorial that Lyn has mentioned. As we settle into the leather seats in his luxury car, he opens up more.

Leaning over, he tells me: 'We have good days and bad days. We still feel his loss, obviously. It never ever goes away. I think it is still very raw for the Taskers. It's extremely hard for military working dogs and dog handlers. When they are going out to Afghanistan, knowing they are going to come under fire, they have to look after and control their dog as well. It's not as if they can just dive for cover; they have their dog to think of.'

I ask him if he thinks dog soldiers, such as his son Ken and pal Liam, get enough credit. He says: 'It's a very specialised role. People have to remember that they are soldiers first and foremost. They do exactly the same job on the ground but they also work with the dogs. It's a really intense environment and the dogs become like comrades, colleagues. When they first started out, the dog unit was just classed as a support unit, now it's a regiment in its own right. When Kenneth was out there, there were only a few dog teams but now they can't get enough of them. There was such demand, Kenneth would go into Kandahar then he would be back out on the ground again. He was in and out all the time.'

We sweep into the car park of a large, white municipal building. The polished, stainless steel sculpture sits on a small mound covered in bright red poppy wreaths. The ten feet high artwork, flanked by heather bushes, was erected in September 2000 by sappers from the Royal Engineers. There are 16 jigsaw pieces with gaps to signify lost loved ones. Two pieces lie on the ground alongside three stainless steel plaques. The centre piece reads 'In memory of those men and women who have made the ultimate sacrifice in the cause of peace since 1945.'

Another plaque to the right says: 'The jigsaw is a metaphor for bereavement, the loss felt at the death of a loved one. It also celebrates family and friends standing together, providing comfort and support into the future.'

A steel plaque in memory of Ken records the fact that he died side by side with Sasha. At the bottom, in black type, are the words: 'Greater love hath no man than this, that a man lay down his life for his friends.' Next to it lies a note from his daughter Hannah saying: 'Daddy, miss you and love you.' His plaque is circled with small wooden crosses emblazoned with a poppy with simple inscriptions from family and friends.

We drive the short distance back to the family home in silence.

I expected this trip to be a depressing experience, the house laden with tragedy and the haunting sadness of a promising life cut short. Few people can hear about the full details of Ken and Sasha's death and not be upset or moved by it in some way. Meeting his family, however, is actually profoundly uplifting. Ken and Sasha are no longer around but their memory is very much alive.

In the Rowe family home, their legacy lives on and will endure for generations. Hannah will grow up hearing tales of her hero dad and his wonder dog. She will listen to how they gave their lives for a better, safer future for kids just like her.

As we arrive back at the family home to say our goodbyes, Lyn takes my arm as I stand on the doorstep. With tears welling in her eyes, she tells me her only consolation is that she knows Ken died doing a job he loved, serving with Sasha.

SIXTEEN

Cairo and the shadowy world of Special Forces

Death would come from the skies. He trotted onto the helicopter and listened intently, ears pricking up at the metallic *thunk* of rifles being cocked and the muffled whine of the engines. It was a moonless evening but he didn't need night vision goggles to make out his surroundings. He saw pretty well in the all-encompassing darkness, unlike his partner sitting behind him, leaning over occasionally to give him a good natured tickle under the chin.

As the helicopter took off, it became clear that this was no ordinary mission. He was on board an ultra-secret helicopter called a Stealth Hawk, a top secret variant of the US Black Hawk chopper. The radar dodging equipment on board and the sleek, angular lines of the chassis were designed to evade tracking by enemy forces.

He was Cairo, a military working dog, tasked with hunting Geronimo. In other words, the US Military's elite Special Forces unit, the US Navy Sea, Air and Land teams, aka US Navy Seals, were deploying their best asset. Cairo was a superbly trained Belgian Malinois, and his mission was to lead the hunt to kill the world's most wanted and hated man, Osama Bin Laden, codename Geronimo.

A military working dog was leading the charge on this most

important mission, dubbed Operation Neptune's Spear. Cairo was heading into the fight with Seal Team Six, an elite within an elite. These human operators are so fit, skilled and experienced they are known as Jedis among the US military, and the unit is classed as a 'black' or secret programme by the US government. It was created in 1980 after the failed attempt to rescue American hostages in Iran, and specialises in counter-terrorism and counter-insurgency operations worldwide.

Former Seal Team Six commander Chuck Pfarrer called the unit 'the United States' principal weapon against terrorism'. One of its unofficial mottos is 'anywhere, anytime'. Screening for Seal Team Six is competitive and by invitation. Only the best Seal operators are allowed to even inquire about the programme. After a lengthy interview process, the most experienced and highly regarded operators are allowed to undergo a rigorous selection course involving one of the world's most punishing training regimes that winnows out all but the best troops.

Cairo and his handler had prepared for hundreds of hours for this mission. They had practiced the raid, time after time, at a segregated section of Camp Alpha at Bagram airfield in Afghanistan in April 2011, using a one acre replica of the compound that intelligence sources believed Bin Laden was hiding in. It had taken ten years of combat, surveillance, interrogation and spy-craft to reach this point.

Now was Cairo's time to shine. As military dog expert Maria Goodavage says: 'You don't have to be a dog lover to be fascinated by the idea that a dog, the cousin of that furry dog begging for scraps under your table, could be one of the heroes who helped execute the most vital and high-tech military mission of the new millennium.'

Details about Cairo's life are sketchy since Special Forces operations are cloaked in secrecy by their respective governments. In the world these forces operate in, everything is very much on a 'need to know' basis and, more often than not, it is deemed that the public don't need to know about how their nation's best operators work. There is even debate about the dog's name, some accounts refer to him as Karo while most call him Cairo.

In the absence of substantiated facts in the aftermath of the raid, rumours about this wonder dog were rife. Some accounts said that he was kitted out like a canine storm trooper with specially adapted night vision goggles and even titanium teeth. Some of these claims, such as the titanium teeth, may be a tad farfetched. Although dogs have indeed been fitted with the metal implants after their own teeth have broken or worn down.

We know that Cairo did have some special kit, however, including bullet proof body armour, a live camera mounted between his shoulders, specially adapted earphones to hear whispered commands and rappelling (abseiling) equipment. He wore a £14,000 K9 Storm Intruder vest, a canine bulletproof flak jacket which was fitted with a live video camera between his shoulders to transmit a dog's eye view back to his handler.

Night vision goggles were not necessary because, like all dogs, Cairo's eyesight improves as it gets darker. He was fitted with a small earbud connected to a wireless transmitter to allow his handler to give whispered commands from hundreds of yards away. He wore doggles, specially designed goggles for dogs, to prevent him being injured by the hailstorm of grit and sand lifted and flung by the helicopter's rotors.

New York Times Bestselling Author Lisa Rogak, who documented the heroism of military dogs in her works 'Dogs of War' and 'Dogs of Courage', detailed the final seconds before Cairo leapt into action: 'As they got closer, the humans got quieter. At one point his handler placed his hands around the dog's vest and shook it, like he was towel drying him after a bath. This was to make sure that there was no noise from anything jangling or moving which could later warn the inhabitants of the compound on which they were zeroing in.'

Stealth was the key to the success of the mission. If Bin Laden and his henchmen knew they the Seals were on their way, he could blow up the compound or stage a last ditch firefight to the death. According to former Seal operator Chuck Pfarrer, who claimed to have unprecedented access to the men who took out Bin Laden, Cairo was part of Red Squadron. This was a special assault unit comprising the most highly decorated troops in the US military.

Each of Cairo's human comrades had at least eight years of combat service under their belts, but Cairo brought his own array of skills to the mission. He was able to carry out a number of tasks including guarding the compound to prevent curious locals from getting too close, alerting his buddies to anyone in the vicinity, and providing bomb detection and tracking roles. If the house was rigged with high explosive booby traps, Cairo would have sniffed them out. He could also have tracked any Al Qaeda gunmen who decided to make a run for it. His hefty bite strength, reportedly seven hundred pounds per square inch, could also have been used to bring down the world's most wanted man should he have bolted from the compound.

Other Special Forces units around the world, use dogs in these multi-skilled roles. One retired British Army handler, who worked with the Special Air Service (SAS), told me: 'These guys tend to use a dog that can play a number of roles, tracking bad guys, providing force protection or even sniffing out weapons and bombs. These dogs are highly skilled just like the operators they work with. The SAS troopers are trained in several skills, whether it's as a demolitions experts or a medic or whatever. Their dogs are just the same, they have to be good enough to be a jack of all trades and a master of them all.'

Cairo's larger than life exploits may sound like the stuff of

Hollywood fantasy but one thing is for certain, he was a real dog and his gallantry was central to the success of the daring raid which killed Bin Laden on May 2 2011. He was considered so vital that President Barack Obama requested a meeting with the four legged warrior after his part in the mission came to light. Obama was at Fort Campbell, Kentucky, to meet the commandos from the raid when he requested some face time with Cairo. The President even got to give him a pat on the head although his muzzle had to stay on at the request of the Secret Service bodyguards.

Cairo is the only member of the raid team, which took on the mission into Bin Laden's hideout in Abbottabad, Pakistan, to be identified so far. The airborne blitz was dubbed 'one of the greatest intelligence and military operations in our nation's history' by President Obama.

Cairo is no canine aberration. He is not a quirky one-off in the ultra-secret stratosphere of military Special Forces where the world's best soldiers operate in a hermetically sealed cocoon with government officials refusing to comment on their methods. On the contrary, working dogs are a vital addition to the already considerable arsenals of many nations' Special Forces, including Britain's shadowy SAS.

Dogs have, in fact, been a central part of airborne operations with British Special Forces since at least World War Two. In the aftermath of D-Day in 1944, soldiers of the Parachute Regiment jumped into the heaviest fighting of the war with dogs by their side. Former Paratrooper Robert Kershaw recorded the phenomena in his book, *Sky Men*. He writes: 'Not every man jumped alone: some dropped with man's best friend, specially trained dogs. "I wonder what has happened to the Alsatian dog and his handler Les Courtell?" reflected Private Sid Capon who had jumped with 9 Para.' These parachuting Alsatians were trained to carry medical equipment and messages. Occasionally, they would hesitate on their first jump but, after being pushed out, they would always follow their handler on later drops.

Sid Capon remembered Les Courtell's dog Glen was used 'to sniff out the Germans' and despite humorous, mischievous attempts by other soldiers to mimic his handler 'he knew only one master'. Glen was affectionately remembered 'as a lovely dog that would jump out of the aeroplane with no assistance from any of the occupants'. Kershaw tells us: 'The dog had its own parachute and when he landed Capon recalled he would 'obediently sit and await his handler when his 'chute had ceased to billow'. Courtell's friends sentimentally recalled 'Glen with his little red light attached to his harness so that his handler could see him. He had to have someone release him, not like us that are capable of doing this ourselves."

Glen was spooked by the battering their aeroplane took from German guns as they approached the Normandy coast, and had to have a 'little help' when it came time to jump into the drop zone. Glen and his handler Les were killed in the hours that followed and their grave can be found at Ranville war cemetery in Normandy with an inscription that reads: 'Glen, the pal of Les.'

Paradog Rob also won fame and glory for his exploits with the SAS during the war although doubts have recently emerged over the true nature of his military career. The black and white collie was reputed to have saved the lives of dozens of soldiers by alerting them to danger as they battled with German forces deep inside occupied Europe and Africa. According to his citation for bravery, Rob, known as War Dog No 471/322, was said to have taken part in twenty parachute jumps in raids in Italy and North Africa during the Second World War.

He was supposedly a real life Lassie who would jump at the first sign of danger, licking the faces of his human comrades to rouse them and warn of lurking enemy forces. Rob's wartime antics, however, may have been a bit more pedestrian. He won the animal version of the Victoria Cross, the Dickin Medal for Gallantry, but his legend was debunked by a former SAS officer.

Professor Quentin Hughes, a former training officer who was awarded the Military Cross and Bar for a daring raid and subsequent escape in Italy, revealed in his autobiography that Rob's tales of derring do were made up after his family wanted him back. His original owners Basil and Heather Bayne had donated him to the Army to help the war effort but were keen to secure his return. SAS troopers had bonded with Rob by this time and created the ruse to keep him. According to this version of events, Rob 'did little more than wag his tail and cheer up ground staff'.

Despite the debate over his wartime antics, Rob was featured in a high profile exhibition at the Imperial War Museum in London and his life formed the basis for a children's book 'Rob the paradog'. Whatever the truth about this remarkable fellow, there is no doubt that dogs play a central part in special operations to this day. Many dogs, who may well have trained alongside Ken Rowe and Sasha at the Defence Animal Centre in Melton Mowbray, are working with UK Special Forces troops such as the SAS and Special Boat Service (SBS).

German Shepherds and Belgian Malinois have been dropped by parachute during missions in Iraq and Afghanistan. Some reports reveal that the dogs have been trained to jump from 25,000 feet with special oxygen masks. These High Altitude High Opening jumps, known by their acronym HAHO, are a Special Forces trademark designed to get forces into hostile territory quickly with little or no noise. High Altitude Low Opening jumps can also be used for elite teams parachuting into enemy held territory in their quest to hunt down what they call High Value Targets: Al Qaeda and Taliban leaders.

Like many military working dogs, such as the German Shepherds at Faslane Naval base in Scotland, these canines are trained to attack anyone carrying a weapon. Dogs were also used in the capture of Saddam Hussein and in the killing of the Iraqi dictator's two sons. Just like Cairo, many of these British dogs have cameras strapped to them as they seek out insurgents. They can more easily evade detection by enemy troops and can access cramped areas that the average soldier cannot.

It is believed that at least eight skyborne dogs have been killed in action working with the SAS between 2001 and 2010. One former Army dog handler said: 'These dogs have to be the best as they are working with top notch soldiers. They are strapped to the handler's chest for the jump. They sometimes have cameras fitted to their harness or just on their heads which send images back to the soldiers as they search buildings, tunnels or whatever it may be.'

Ministry of Defence officials always remain tight-lipped about operations involving the SAS and other Special Forces units. But former Prime Minister Gordon Brown revealed there were 500 British special forces operating in Afghanistan and Tony Blair praised them in his autobiography 'A Journey'. General David Petraeus, commander of US and NATO-led forces in Afghanistan, has also been outspoken in his praise of his elite forces.

SAS troops, with specialist units such as Task Force Black, were very active in Iraq tracking down Saddam Hussein's henchmen. They were deployed in 'kill or capture' missions against al-Qaeda fanatics and Saddam's inner circle. Since British troops left Iraq, they have now focussed solely on Afghanistan with their marine comrades from the SBS.

Recent newspaper reports claimed that British Special Forces and their dogs had 'decapitated' the Taliban leadership in Helmand and Kandahar provinces. One account said: 'The SAS was killing Taliban fighters in Helmand on an 'industrial scale' with a quarter of senior commanders, several hundred, dead since the spring. Petraeus has said UK and US Special Forces were fighting at an unprecedented tempo in Afghanistan.'

This growing use of dogs by British and US forces has not been without its critics. Animal rights campaigners have condemned their deployment in warzones, claiming that humans have no right to put the dogs' lives at risk. A statement from People for the Ethical Treatment of Animals (PETA) said: 'Dogs are not tools or 'innovations' and are not ours to use and toss away like empty shells.'

Soldiers though, do not see their dogs as mere equipment, to be used and discarded. A symbol of the deep, abiding bond between the warriors of the SAS and their war dogs can be seen at the crack regiment's headquarters near Hereford. A modest stone memorial features a black engraving of the famed SAS emblem or cap badge of Excalibur pointing downward, wreathed in flames and often colloquially referred to as a winged dagger.

Next to this image sits a portrait etched in metal of a proud looking German Shepherd, mouth open, his eyes gazing out at passers by. This memorial marks the lives of two hero hounds who died fighting with members of 'The Regiment' as the SAS is known. German Shepherds Thor and Scotty were killed in action on secret missions in Iraq. Soldiers erected the monument in a garden at the regiment's HQ Stirling Lines. Below the SAS insignia and the picture, sits a plaque emblazoned with the Latin motto *Semper Vigilo, Fortis, Paratus et Fidelis* – 'Always vigilant, strong, prepared and faithful'.

Both dogs died in 2008 as SAS operators fought to the death to destroy a network of Al-Qaeda bombers. They raced into buildings to take down insurgents who were determined to escape the clutches of the SAS. Thor grabbed an Al-Qaeda fighter's leg, refusing to let go despite being shot three times and hacked with a machete. He was later put down due to his injuries. Six months previously, Scotty was shot dead on a night-time mission.

The tribute to the two dogs is not as well-known as the SAS clock tower memorial in Hereford, a simple, unadorned structure crowned with a large, square block at the top with a white clock face so stark it is not even marked with numerals to mark the hours.

Halfway up the tower, onlookers can just make out the SAS cap badge. An inscription on the base is a moving verse from 'The Golden Road to Samarkand' by James Elroy Flecker which is memorised by the regiment's soldiers. Its words emphasise bravery, perseverance and indomitable will, qualities that are vital for SAS soldiers and traits that Thor and Scotty showed too:

> We are the Pilgrims, master; we shall go
> Always a little further: it may be
> Beyond that last blue mountain barred with snow
> Across that angry or that glimmering sea . . .

One soldier said: 'Thor and Scotty were with us through thick and thin in Iraq and never let us down. They won't be forgotten.'

SEVENTEEN

Re-united at last

Memphis hesitates, snuffles along the ground, looking slightly unsure of himself. Then, blissfully, in an instant, he runs over and jumps into Mick's arms. The months of application forms, phone calls and sleepless nights are finally over. Mick has Memphis back. This time, he is never going to let him go.

It has been a long road to get to this reunion. Mick suffers from horrific injuries that would shatter the lives of lesser men. In months to come, he will have his leg amputated below the knee. In some ways, though, he is a lucky man. He was on the receiving end of the biggest killer in Afghanistan, the IED, and yet he survived. Many will not be so fortunate.

He will bear the scars of the day he was blown up forever but, at least from now on, he will have his best buddy Memphis by his side. Following his period of recovery at Headley Court rehab centre, he finally met his four-legged pal at an RAF base. Mick's voice trembles at the memory of the pair's reunion: 'It was brilliant to see him again. He came bounding down and eventually recognised me. It was such a relief to see him after such a long time.'

He is grateful that his role and battle to recover from his injuries is helping to raise awareness of how vital RAF dog teams are to the British campaign. He says: 'The Channel 5 programme in particular was fantastic, it's really showed what the guys are doing on the ground. It was very realistic. The morning after the programme went out, the nurses were wanting to know what was happening to Memphis. Everyone recognises you and comes in saying 'I saw your face on the telly'. It's quite good to get recognition for the RAF as loads of people don't even know we are on the front-line.'

Despite his brush with death, working with Memphis is one of the best experiences of his life. It may be hard for civilians to understand, but Mick does not regret a minute of his life on the frontline with Memphis: 'There is nothing like it. I was sent out to Checkpoint Toki because the marines had lost so many guys to IEDs. They appreciated the dog being with them not just for the IEDs and weapons caches but because it broke the monotony, they could play with him. It was something different to get them through the daily grind.'

Mick explains that the relationship between dog and soldiers is so profoundly important that often, when human and canine fail to gel as a team, they have to go their separate ways. The dog is as much an independent player in the bonding process as the soldier. If Fido doesn't like you, then it's time to hit the road and find another partner. Mick says 'The team has to work because if you and the dog don't get on, you are not working to your full potential. Being Scottish, with my accent, I would never handle a bitch because my voice is too strong. I would normally get a hard dog because my voice is strong and forceful. I would keep the dog in check so that he knows the pecking order. It's all about teamwork. That's the key to it.'

If a handler doesn't get on with his dog things can go wrong very quickly. The dog will ignore him, putting lives in danger or assets at risk. Mick tells me that, with any search or patrol dog, the first thing he does is take him out of the kennel for two minutes, then put him back before repeating the process over and over. He says: 'It's that act of getting him out of the kennel, the dogs thinks "oh, this guy is giving me something good, he's being nice to me".'

There were no bonding problems between Mick and Memphis. The pair connected instantly. Mick has an endearing, infectious laugh that erupts as he remembers how quickly they both hit it off. His partnership with Memphis came about purely by chance after he didn't connect with another dog, Sam. Mick compares the bonding process to the intimacy of a parent and child relationship. The dog thinks 'daddy is looking after me'.

He says: 'With Memphis it was only about a week because we really hit it off. You have to turn the dog down sometimes. I took a dog out from the UK with me; called Sam. He was a little Spaniel but it was the weirdest thing, once he got to Afghanistan he didn't want to listen to me. He was a dog that needed a soft handler with a softer voice and softer mannerisms.'

Sam was given to another soldier and Mick was given Memphis. In no time, Mick and Memphis were in huge demand as a first class dog team and, thanks to their top talents, they got to work with the aristocracy of the British military. As an impartial RAF 'bod' Mick is perfectly placed to compare the pros and cons of the elite units.

I asked him which of the famous regiments and corps had been the best to work with. He served with a glittering array of prestigious units from 4 SCOTS, The Highlanders, 5 SCOTS, The Argyll and Sutherland Highlanders, to 2 PARA, the Brigade Reconnaissance Force and the Afghan National Army, and Memphis was always a great icebreaker.

He says: 'You get the dog in there and you let the troops play with him and it helps to breaks the monotony for the soldiers.' Each infantry unit has its own way of working, each is a band of warriors with its own foibles and rituals, according to Mick. Everyone, however, was glad to see Memphis ambling round their base: 'When we were in fire fights, people would go out of their way to look out for me. My first enemy contact was with 5 SCOTS. They just got on top of me, dealt with it and we got out of there. They tend to recruit from the west of Scotland, my stomping ground, so it was good working with people from my local town.'

Mick says he really had to work hard to prove his worth to the Royal Marines, the troops he was serving with when he was injured. 'After the first couple of patrols, they will see you as part of their team. It is important that you show that you are not just a hanger on. It's the Green Beret mentality. The Paras were ace as well. That was my first mission, we went out to Checkpoint Shabarak. They are pretty switched on guys. They appreciated Memphis and what he could do. I did my first helicopter assault with them. That was hugely exhilarating.'

Looking back, Mick enjoyed every aspect of his Afghan experience alongside Memphis. He smiles, remembering how Memphis grew to love sprinting on and off helicopters. Mick would walk him to the landing pad as helicopters landed and took off. He would play with him, offering reassurance, as the powerful backdraft from the rotor blades washed over them. Memphis is a seasoned veteran, he was deployed on his third tour when Mick was hurt, notching up a total of 18 months in action in Afghanistan. Dogs like him can start working when they are as young as two or three-years-old. Depending on the dog, they can be retired at around nine-years-old.

Over time, Memphis even became nonchalant about the sudden, violent roar of gunfights. 'At first, he would come and sit beside me, looking a bit nervous and shaking a wee bit but after five minutes he would be up and working away. That's what the guys need to see. You really don't need a dog that's scared or broken for the rest of the day.'

At the ripe old age of 37, Mick was considered the Grandad

of each unit. Some of the soldiers Mick worked with were in their late teens or early twenties. His advancing years and more genteel RAF experience meant he had to work hard to keep up with tough infantry troops in Afghanistan.

He spent months raising his fitness to the required standard, and so did Memphis: 'I am a lot older than many of the guys so that was a difficulty. It was mega hard on the fitness side. I wasn't used to tabbing or carrying weight or stuff like that so I spent five months in pre-deployment training just to get ready to go out on tour.'

During his pre-deployment training, Mick was up each dawn to go for a run with Memphis, although the searing heat meant he couldn't continue this regimen on operations. On his tour, Mick often had to lift Memphis over eight feet walls. He would grab his harness and lift him up to a waiting soldier on the roof.

This intense physical job has undoubtedly left its mark on Mick but the invisible scars of war often go much deeper, even in dogs. Psychologists have documented the effects of the stress of combat on humans, but dogs are intelligent and sensitive enough to be deeply shaken by the incredible ferocity of the modern battlefield. Memphis is one such victim of the war in Afghanistan, and had to be retired after witnessing his beloved daddy being blown up.

Mick says: 'If Memphis had been there next to me it might not have happened. I think if he had gone over the IED; he would have got it. I went away in the helicopter and the marines took him back to Checkpoint Toki. One of the other dog handlers fetched him back to Bastion that night. He was retired then and there, since he had been through a big shock and they didn't want to put him with someone else. My unit was due to come back from Afghan so he had done enough.'

Memphis was taken back to kennels in Germany for his quarantine before being reunited with his daddy at RAF

Waddington. Their long awaited first meeting must have been a heart-warming sight. The six-year-old black and white Spaniel went into a tail wagging frenzy once he realised who had come to visit. 'It was brilliant to see him again. He just came bounding out the room, had a run round the compound and eventually recognised me. It was a good day. Once I am properly on my feet, I will have to get up and walk him so we will keep each other going. I will never run again but I will walk again.'

In 2013, doctors had to amputate Mick's damaged foot. His extreme pain meant below the knee amputation was his only option. News of the severity of his injuries had, at first, been a shock to his family. They thought he had a safe rear echelon job. Miles from the nearest battlefield or Taliban fighter. Little did they know, he was out on the front-line all day, every day.

He says: 'To save my parents from worrying, I told them I was working as a drugs dog handler in an air terminal, searching passengers and stuff like that. They had no idea I was front line with the marines. It was a bit of a shock to them when they found out. They were grateful that I was in the best place in the best hands. They knew I was being very well looked after.'

His amputation came after months of training and physiotherapy at Headley Court to help him retain his mobility. At home, Mick now uses crutches for short walks and a wheelchair for longer distances. He grapples every day to rebuild his life. His prime motivator remains the thought of enjoying his time relaxing at home with Memphis. He says: 'I just couldn't wait to get Memphis by the fire and get him well and truly spoiled. He is one spoiled dog. My fiancée Lorna loves him to bits so it's great. She has always been a dog lover but I had to get the go ahead from her to have him in the house. She loves him and he's such a good house pet as well.'

Despite his terrible toll of injuries, Mick is adamant that nothing compares to those days with Memphis wading through ditches, trudging across fields and clambering over compounds to defeat the Taliban bomb makers. They shared the ultimate, unspoken bond of trust. He insists that working dogs are the most effective military asset today, not just for IEDs but for morale as well.

He trusts Memphis with his life: 'People ask me what level of reassurance I can give that the dog is working. If the dog has been over a piece of ground, I will go over it. I trusted Memphis implicitly then and I still do now. I will never have job satisfaction like that in my life again. It was fantastic just knowing you can help keep guys safe. I was in a handful of firefights. That was more than enough. One was enough, to be honest.'

Mick sums up his experience with Memphis best in his own diary. He is proud to have shown that RAF men and women have as good a record of service in Afghanistan as has any other branch of Britain's armed forces. He knows he will never see action on the front-line again but, as he ruffles Memphis's ear, he can be proud that his comrades and their dogs continue to save lives.

Civilians will never know what it's like to pat their dog on the head for one last time, before heading out into the badlands to save others and stare death in the face. Mick acknowledges the difficult truth that, in future, he will never have the same job satisfaction he had with Memphis. In a wistful tone, he says: 'I am just happy to have shown what we are capable of.'

Epilogue

A shocking video emerged on the internet, highlighting the risks to hundreds of canines at work in Afghanistan, as I completed this book in February 2014. My heart felt heavy as I watched the footage of a terrified Belgian Shepherd being paraded before a video camera by his Taliban captors. The dog, believed to have been deployed with British Special Forces, looked tired and subdued as it was displayed by a group of long haired insurgents.

The shaky footage moved around the forlorn looking animal before focussing on other spoils of war including captured weapons. Images of the dog, panting nervously as it eyed his new owners, have been seared into my mind. This video yet again emphasised that military working dogs serve us just as much as their two legged comrades.

Thousands of people around the world viewed the amateur video after it was published on an Islamic militant website. Military sources reportedly disputed claims that the dogs was American, saying he was a British dog working with the SAS. It wears an expensive shoulder harness so he can be hoisted quickly in and out of helicopters and across difficult terrain. Thankfully, he looked well fed and had no obvious signs of mistreatment.

A Taliban spokesman said the dog was captured by

fighters during a raid in the Laghman province east of Kabul on December 23. Pentagon officials corroborated the story saying the dog was believed to have been captured around that time. This date tallies with a major British mission to the east of Kabul during which Captain Richard Holloway of the Royal Engineers, was killed. Ministry of Defence officials refused to comment although a spokesman for the NATO-led International Security Assistance Force confirmed that a dog had gone missing in December.

This, sadly, wasn't the first time that the Taliban had captured a hero dog, using her for their own calculating propaganda. In 2010, an Australian bomb-sniffing dog was lost in Afghanistan and adopted by a Taliban leader who tried to sell her back. Sabi, a black Labrador, was eventually recovered by an American Special Forces soldier who retrieved her in north-eastern Oruzgan.

I just hoped that this captured dog would live to see happier days. Some dogs suffer horrendous injuries in Afghanistan but go on to live fulfilled, productive lives, spending their days continuing to serve their human buddies. In the US, Yeager is one such wounded hero who encapsulates the sacrifice and honour of these magnificent animals.

Seven-year-old black Labrador Yeager has completed two tours of duty in Afghanistan and one in Iraq, uncovering a toll of than 100 improvised explosive devices. This hero saved countless lives and has been awarded two Purple Heart medals. However, he suffered a massive blow in April 2012 when his handler Lance Corporal Abraham Tarwoe was killed by a roadside bomb in Afghanistan.

Yeager suffered serious injuries in the blast. Shrapnel ripped through his nose and chest and he lost part of his ear. The physical trauma though was nothing compared to Yeager's devastation at the loss his 'daddy'. In heartbreaking scenes at Tarwoe's memorial service, the dog lay down beside the

Marine's cross and would not move. Even in death, the pair were inseparable. The United States Marine Corps motto of *Semper Fi* or Always Faithful had never been more apt.

Now, as Yeager struggles to overcome his own physical and emotional wounds, he has also been helping fellow human veterans on the road to recovery. As Marine Sergeant David Tupper recuperates from combat-related injuries he suffered in Afghanistan, Yeager has become his constant canine companion.

Tupper said: 'They had to pull him away from Tarwoe's memorial service. Since he was also injured, it was kind of like a two-way street. He lost his handler, but was also going through recovery with it. The day I went to receive him, he wouldn't leave my side. He climbed into the passenger seat into my lap.'

Yeager is a source of limitless emotional support but he also helps Tupper to carry out practical tasks around the home: 'He helps me through the doors if it's a tight squeeze. He'll get on my lap if we're going down a hill and kind of make sure I'm not going too fast. He gets worried. Recently, kayaking, when I'm doing flips, he gets real nervous and tries to get in the water to come to me.' It is hard to quantify the value of Yeager and his four legged comrades for soldiers on the frontline and, indeed, for veterans still battling their own demons on the home front.

Back in the UK, bracketed between stories about the opening of a new plumbers' merchant and warnings of a spate of catalytic converter thefts, I noticed a modest article detailing a bid to raise a monument to Britain's four legged heroes. Melton Mowbray's local newspaper highlighted the quest of animal lovers to raise £40,000 to build a series of sculptures in the town.

The bronze statues of a German Shepherd on guard, an alert Labrador and a leaping Springer Spaniel will be erected in front of Melton Council's offices. As the nerve centre for our country's military working dogs, Melton is the logical place to pay tribute to these wonderful animals and the dedicated soldiers who fight alongside them. The sculpture will go at least some of the way towards giving soldiers dogs and handlers the credit they so obviously deserve.

As the conflict in Afghanistan grinds to a close, however, after more than 13 years, longer than the First and Second World Wars combined, the contribution of dogs is in danger yet again of being overlooked. In 2012, the US Senate passed a law classifying military working dogs as full members of the armed forces. They were judged to be more than just military equipment.

This historic piece of legislation means that when there are no suitable adoptions available for a dog that is due to retire, he or she will be transferred to a training unit until a home can be found for them. The bill also sets out measures to cover veterinary care and transport fees, including flying dogs home from a warzone. A telling paragraph in the bill also demands 'a decoration or other appropriate recognition to recognize such dogs that are killed in action or perform an exceptionally meritorious or courageous act during their service.'

No such move is being planned in Britain. I met handlers who were appalled that furry comrades, who faced blizzards of bullets and fields of IEDs at their side, were still technically classed as equipment with their own NATO stock number. This means dogs are technically just classed as another piece of stock like ammunition boxes or camp beds. Much to the chagrin of combat hardened handlers, many people still see working with dogs as a 'rear echelon' job for soldiers patrolling bases well away from the frontline. Nothing could be further from the truth.

Dogs like Sasha, Memphis, Benji, Theo, Harry and all their kennel mates save soldiers every day. It is difficult to even begin to evaluate their outstanding bravery and their silent, obedient service to their country. How do you calculate how many soldiers' legs or eyes they have saved, the number of troops lives they have preserved?

It is time we took a leaf from the USA's book by giving these dogs some long overdue recognition and formal protection after they have served their country. When the war in Afghanistan ends and Britain's troops return home for the last time, they will bring with them hundreds of military working dogs who will often also bear the physical and mental scars of their service. We owe them so much. It is our duty to ensure they are looked after and their devotion and sacrifice is remembered alongside that of their human brothers and sisters in arms.

Perhaps though, things are changing for the better in the UK. As this book was receiving its final edits, Ken Rowe's remarkable dog Sasha received the highest recognition for her bravery in Afghanistan, the PDSA Dickin Medal – the animal Victoria Cross. Truly well deserved but it is heart rending that the award must be posthumous. Her citation reads: 'Sasha's determination to search and push forward – despite gruelling conditions and relentless Taliban attacks – was a morale boost to the soldiers who entrusted their lives to her weapon-finding capability. On one occasion, recalled by regimental colleagues, Sasha was searching a building in Garmsir when she detected two mortars and a large quantity of weaponry, including explosives and mines. This find alone undoubtedly saved the lives of many soldiers and civilians.'

Heroes come in all shapes, sizes AND species. Just because some of our soldiers bark and chase cats does not mean they can't be heroes too. They are our true glory hounds.

Select Bibliography

BOOKS

A Dog's Purpose by W. Bruce Cameron. Pan, London 2011.

Afgantsy: The Russians in Afghanistan 1979–1989 by Rodric Braithwaite. Oxford University Press, London 2012.

A Home of Their Own: The heart-warming 150 year history of Battersea Dogs & Cats Home by Garry Jenkins. Bantam, London 2011.

A Million Bullets: The real story of the British Army in Afghanistan by James Fergusson. Corgi, London 2009.

Animals in War by Jilly Cooper. Corgi London 1984.

An Ordinary Soldier: Afghanistan. A Ferocious Enemy. A Bloody Conflict. One Man's Impossible Mission by Doug Beattie. Pocket Books, London 2009.

Aviation Assault Battle Group: The 2009 Afghanistan Tour of The Black Watch. Pen & Sword Aviation, London 2011.

Beyond the Call of Duty by Isabel George. Harper, London 2010.

Bomb Hunters: In Afghanistan with Britain's Elite Bomb Disposal Unit by Sean Rayment. Collins, London 2011.

British War Dogs: Their training and psychology by Lieutenant Colonel Edwin Hautonville Richardson. Skeffington & Son, London 1920. (Published online at http://archive.org/stream/britishwardogsth00richrich#page/n5/mode/2up).

Dead Men Risen: The Welsh Guards and the Real Story of Britain's War in Afghanistan by Toby Harnden. Quercus, London 2011.

Dog Heroes: True Stories of Canine Courage by Ben Holt. Summersdale, London 2009.

Dogs at War by Blythe Hamer. Carlton, London 2001.

Ground Truth: 3 Para Return to Afghanistan by Patrick Bishop. HarperPress, London 2010.

In Defence of Dogs by John Bradshaw. Allen Lane, London 2011.

Inside the Elite Forces by Nigel Cawthorne. Robinson, London 2008.

It's All About Treo: Life and War with the World's Bravest Dog by Dave Heyhoe. Quercus 2012.

Little America: The War within the War for Afghanistan by Rajiv Chandrasekaran. Bloomsbury, London 2012.

Military Working Dogs. Field manual. Department of Defence, Pentagon Publishing 2005.

No Place Like Home: A New Beginning with the Dogs of Afghanistan by Pen Farthing. Ebury, London 2011.

191

One Dog at a Time: Saving the Strays of Helmand by Pen Farthing. Ebury, London 2010.

Operation Snakebite: The Explosive True Story of an Afghan Desert Siege by Stephen Grey. Penguin, London 2010.

Seal Target Geronimo: The Inside Story of the mission to kill Osama Bin Laden by Chuck Pfarrer. Quercus, London 2011.

Sky Men: Always Expect the Unexpected – the Real Story of the Paras by Robert Kershaw. Hodder & Stoughton, London 2010.

Soldier Dogs: The Untold Story of America's Canine Heroes by Maria Goodavage. Dutton, New York 2012.

Soldier: The Autobiography by General Sir Mike Jackson. Corgi, London 2008.

Stumbling Bear: Soviet Military Performance in Afghanistan by Scott R McMichael. Brassey's UK. London, 1991.

Taliban by James Fergusson. Bantam Press, London 2010.

The Dogs of War by Lisa Rogak. St Martin's Griffin, New York 2012.

The Hidden War by Artyom Borovik. Faber and Faber, London 2001.

The Junior Officers' Reading Club: Killing Time and Fighting Wars by Patrick Hennessey. Penguin, London, 2010.

The Official British Army Fitness Guide, Guardian Books, London 2009.

The Outpost: An Untold Story of American Valor by Jake Tapper. Little, Brown and Co. 2012.

3 Para by Patrick Bishop. HarperPress, London 2007.

War by Sebastian Junger. Fourth Estate, London 2011.

WEBSITES

A biography of EH Richardson http://community-2.webtv.net/Hahn-50thAPK9/K9History13/

BBC news: www.bbc.co.uk/news/

Defence Focus www.mod.uk/DefenceInternet/DefenceNews/InDepth/DefenceFocus.htm

Desider – magazine for Defence Equipment and Support www.mod.uk/DefenceInternet/MicroSite/DES/OurPublications/desider/Index.htm

Duke Canine Cognition Centre http://evolutionaryanthropology.duke.edu/research/dogs

Ministry of Defence: www.mod.uk

Science magazine www.sciencemag.org

Soldier magazine: www.army.mod.uk/soldier-magazine/soldiermagazine.aspx

The Daily Record: www.dailyrecord.co.uk

The Daily Telegraph: www.telegraph.co.uk

The Dog's Sense of Smell http://www.aces.edu/pubs/docs/U/UNP-0066/UNP-0066.pdf

The Guardian: www.guardian.co.uk

The New York Times: www.nytimes.com

The Sun: www.thesun.co.uk

UK Forces in Afghanistan blog: http://ukforcesafghanistan.wordpress.com/

Victoria Stilwell Positively http://positively.com/

TV/FILM

Royal Marines: Mission Afghanistan. Director Chris Terrill.

War Dogs of the Pacific. Director Harris Done.

Index

Photographs are noted as '*caption page – number*' in *italics*, and the names of military working dogs in **Bold**

Index

Index

Index

Index

201